MICHAEL KELLY

MOTHERS
OF THE CITY

TWENTY
OUTSTANDING
LIVERPOOL WOMEN

$\mathscr{D}$edication

To my Daughter Diane and my Grand-daughters

Published by
AJH Publishing
54 Brows Lane
Formby
L37 4ED

Printed by
Ribcar
56 Lower Breck Road
Tuebrook, Liverpool
L6 4BZ

Contents

Foreword

Well, here we have the stories of Michael Kelly's women and that should bring a wee smile and raise a quizzical eyebrow or two in the hushed halls of learning, where the man himself now steps in his soft-soled shoes. This is a chap who saw history unfold in the poor areas of his city. Although his first calling was woodwork, he became the teller of true stories and that made him an historian as well. Of course, his sympathy lay with those who had given of themselves. And why not? He had no time for the greedy and those who placed their ambition before the needs of others. So his history comes from the heart. That is why his words are now read and heard in places far from his own upbringing in the Kirkdale district. It is a privilege to call Michael a friend, this true Liverpudlian with a smiling face squeezed from the moss of his ancestral Ireland. The truth is that Michael cares about his book and he wants you to enjoy it.

David Charters
feature writer and columnist
The Liverpool Daily Post.
14.11.2007

Acknowledgements

en years ago the idea of writing a book on some of the outstanding women of Liverpool had never entered my head. It was after the publication of 'The Life and Times of Kitty Wilkinson' appeared on the bookshelves that I was continually asked about writing the story of other Liverpool and Merseyside women. It is those people I wish to thank, for encouraging and helping me to continue and finish this project.

I wish to thank Hilary King for her great support in this project and for putting me in touch with Glenys Konrad, daughter of Ethel Austin, and to Glenys for giving me access to family records and photographs. I wish to thank Rosemary Morris for editing this work and for her valuable advice and great patience. My thanks to Margaret Graham, for all her help and advice, and Marie McQuade, for her support and allowing me to delve into her research work on family history. My thanks to David Charters, journalist and columnist with the 'Liverpool Daily Post', for his wonderful support in highlighting my work in his newspaper. My thanks to Ron Formby, editor of the Scottie Press, a community newspaper, for his support in promoting my work and for being the best community worker I know.

My thanks to my friend, Cheniston K. Roland, violin and music historian, for encouraging me in this work and for his photographic skills. To the staff of the Liverpool Athenaeum library for all their tremendous help in my hour of need. The staff of Liverpool Central Library who are always prepared to go that step further in helping in my research, and the staff of Crosby Sefton Library. To the staff of The National Library of Ireland, Dublin, and 'The Irish Post' newspaper for publishing my article on Kitty Wilkinson.

I am indebted to artist Anthony Brown, art director 'Emso Illustration Fine Art Design', for supporting and encouraging me in my work and for being a good friend. My thanks to 'Ireland's Own' a wonderful family magazine, for publishing some of my previous work on outstanding Liverpool women. I wish to thank my friend Olwen McLaughlin from Editions Limited (art gallery) for her encouragement and support. Also I wish to thank John Kerrigan, a fighter of good causes, for his reminiscences of Bessie Braddock.

My thanks to Ray Fiske, Phil Finegan of Ribcar for his patience and support, also Hilary King, Eileen Kelly and Jane Aeron.

Introduction

The object of the following pages is to give a glimpse of the lives of those who have spent their days helping and aiding the poor in poverty and distress, and in making the world a brighter place by their actions. They are women who have lived on this earth whom we regard at times as being in the past, nothing to do with us, 'gone and dusted', as the saying goes. We sometimes feel there is little or no place for those who graced the streets of Liverpool with their presence in an age gone by. However, they are the foundation stone on which this society stands, together with all the things we take for granted. The history of their lives is, at times, more thrilling than some of the fictional stories that take up most of the room on the shelves of our great libraries and bookstores. They showed us the way to good health and education, and we can still learn from them. Looking back even further, we still learn from the ancient Greeks and Romans about modern living, from Shakespeare about the beauty of language. We look back when it suits us, and the memories of the past are always present. Margaret Simey, in her 'Josephine Butler Memorial Lecture' reminds us of the way we view Josephine.

Books are written about her as a forgotten saint, all very noble and uplifting but nothing to do with us. I believe that this attitude to Josephine is typical of the blind refusal to look back before we try to move forward, that is a major cause of our current loss of direction. We never seem to learn. The capacity of the human race to go on re-inventing the wheel never ceases to amaze me. In fact, Josephine is no saint who from her labours rests. What she did and why she did it is of a fundamental importance, which makes it of direct relevance to the social and political turbulence in which we find ourselves today, and even more to the unforeseeable future, which we nervously contemplate.

Josephine Butler was a champion of women's rights in the early days of the suffragette movement. This in 1866 was when oppressive laws curtailed women's rights. She visited workhouses and witnessed poor women being subjected to what could only be regarded as forced labour in the oakum sheds. In the field of law we have Dame Rose Heilbron, a woman who by her very presence must have inspired trust and reassurance, a woman who rose to the top of her profession and was admired by her peers in a world dominated by men. She must have been an inspiration to women in all walks of life.

Bessie Braddock M.P. stood up to the best legal minds in the House of Commons when she was fighting for the rights of those in her constituency who lived in sub-standard housing. She was not afraid to tell the dockers, when they were out on strike, "You leave it to me and I will sort your problem out", and they would trust Bessie to help them and went back to work.

In education, Liverpool was blessed by having Jessie Reid Crosbie, a teacher and headmistress of outstanding ability. She used her school to put into place many of the benefits we all enjoyed, such as milk and she tried to improve the lives of the families.

When we think of sport, we are often reminded of a football player who is never off the sports pages of the national press, but he has ten other players to help him on the field. The achievements of Charlotte (Lottie) Dod appears to have had no equal in the United Kingdom, as she was a superb athlete. Starting at the age of 11 she went on to win Wimbledon 5 times, but she also rose to the heights of other leading sports. We have had some great athletes but none to compare with Charlotte (Lottie) Dod.

In business, Ethel Austin showed by example that if you have a dream you can achieve anything with enough determination. She lived in a council house when she opened her first wool business, and went on to build an empire of shops. Three women, from different backgrounds, showed the way to improve public health; they were Kitty Wilkinson, Nurse Agnes Jones and Margaret Beaven.

Liverpool also had its poets, and Felicia Dorothea Hemans was a good example of one, but she was more than that, she was outstanding. She loved the beauty of the English language, and she could paint pictures with words when she constructed a poem. 'Casabianca', was perhaps her most well known work, also known as 'The Boy Stood on the Burning Deck'

Some may not have a direct input into the future but inspire us to succeed, and quite often we take things for granted, never querying how the benefits of modern society came about.

Chapter 1

Dame Rose Heilbron

Liverpool in the 1950s was still in a sorry state, recovering from the war years. The town had plenty of entertainers and sporting heroes but more than that was needed - someone who stood head and shoulders above the rest, a person with great intellectual ability, handsome and beautiful, a model that war weary people could all look up to, a sort of Greek Goddess, and this role was filled by Rose Heilbron, She came to the notice of the general public when she was the defending Barrister in a famous Liverpool murder trail.

Rose was born on the 19 August 1914, into a Jewish family in Liverpool where her father had a boarding house for immigrant refugees. He prospered and took over a small hotel, in which his daughters were expected to help, but Rose's elder sister, Anne, who married a foundry worker, did most of the housework. "Let Rose get on with her studying", said her mother Nellie, who also ensured that her younger daughter had elocution lessons. Nellie sadly died in 1938.

From Belvedere School, Rose went to Liverpool University,

graduating with a first-class honours degree in law in 1935 and in 1937 she took her Masters degree in law. Two years later she was called to the Bar and joined the northern circuit, of which she would become leader in 1973.

Almost everything in the notable career of Dame Rose Heilbron was a first. One of the outstanding defence barristers of the post-war period, she was the first woman to win the Lord Justice Holber's scholarship to Gray's Inn, the first woman to be appointed silk, the first to lead in a murder case, the first woman recorder, the first woman to sit at the Old Bailey and the first woman treasurer of Gray's Inn.

Rose soon fell under the eye of the Recorder of Liverpool, E.G. Hemmerde, who had led for the Crown in the famous Liverpool case of William Wallace, who was accused of killing his wife but released by the Court of Appeal on the grounds of an unsafe conviction. Hemmerde made a special point of welcoming Heilbron on her first appearance before him, and expressed the hope she would return, as she was, for some time, an isolated female figure in Northern Courts.

In 1945, Rose married the Dublin born Nathaniel Burstein, whom she met at Court. He became a consultant at a Liverpool hospital, and there is little doubt that the proximity of medical knowledge was of great help to her in the Bloom case, where a manslaughter verdict was returned, and Bloom was given three years. After the trial, a fan wrote, "Dear lady, you can't go around persuading juries that men are entitled to strangle their lady friends".

Those jealous of her career said that she benefited from the fact that, for her first six years, so many able men were in the armed forces. Given the prejudices of the Bar at the time, there is little doubt that, without the second world war, she would have faced more limitations, but her meteoric rise once the men were back proved that she was head and shoulders above most of her contemporaries. A Liverpool journalist of the time recalls, "She got up there by sheer hard work and cleverness." Rose won her first murder trial acquittal, at the age of 29 in 1946 and in the same year she appeared in 10 murder trials. Three years later, she and Helena Normanton, nearly twice her age, became the first women King's Council.

In the 1950s, Rose became something of a household name to the crime-loving public, and a queen to her home city. In 1949-50 she became the first woman to lead in a English murder case, when she defended George Kelly, accused of shooting dead the deputy manager of the Cameo cinema in Liverpool. He is reputed to have said "he wasn't having a Judy defend him". For the appearances in five appeals on his behalf, and speaking 150,000 words in the process, Heilbron received the princely sum of 15 guineas, which led to her being named the Daily Mirror's 'Woman of the Year'. She was unable to save Kelly from the gallows (though in 2003 the court of appeal quashed his conviction as unsafe). But her successes in the first half of the 1950s included the defence of four men accused of hanging a boy during a burglary. She was able to show the death was an accident, as was that of the Hartlepool solicitor, Louis Bloom, who was accused of murdering his mistress in his office.

In 1951, Rose successfully defended Anna Neary, also accused of murdering a woman in her bath. The following year, her client Mary Standish walked free from court after standing trial for the murder of her husband. Another client, the Knowsley Hall footman, escaped the gallows on the grounds of insanity after shooting two men dead and seriously wounding the Countess of Derby in the smoking room of her stately home. Rose Heilbron's bold decision to call a psychiatrist as the only defence witness was considered a masterstroke. Another success was Freeman Reese, a black deserter from the American Army, who was acquitted of murdering a policeman in Burton-Upon-Trent.

When she appeared at the Old Bailey in 1951, defending Liverpool dockers accused of incitement to strike, the newspapers announced that she received £750 and £150 a day, then the highest brief fee paid to a woman, but it was well earned. The Attorney General, Sir Hartley (later Lord) Shawcross, withdrew the case shortly before it was to go to the jury. Articles began to quote Heilbron's earnings as more than £5,000 a year, and reported on the family house, said to be worth "over £5,000", in which she, her husband and daughter Hilary, lived.

Rose had become a Liverpool celebrity and when she went to America for the Bar Conference, and took the salute as Honorary Colonel of the East Lancashire Battalion of the Womens Royal

Army Core (WRAC) she was reported to have been the first woman in Liverpool to wear a calf-length evening dress. This made news for she was not known to have a flair for fashion, generally dressing sensibly rather than flamboyantly, but local outfitters knew they 'could not sell Rose poor quality garments'. She was a very beautiful woman in her youth, and she retained her good looks.

Rose was soon wanted for all major cases. It was rumoured she would defend Christopher Craig in the 1953 case in which he and Derek Bentley were accused of killing a policeman, but she did not do so. However, she did defend Violet Wright, accused in 1956 of setting fire to a Essex houseboat, which resulted in the death of her twin sons. Heilbron succeeded, in part due to the customs of the time, in persuading the jury that Wright would not have put her hair in curlers knowing that she would meet the Fire Brigade. A fellow lawyer said of her, "She defends a person more than a set of facts. I think it shows that she is a woman and that helps her." The London gang leader, Jack Spot Comer, whom Heilbron successfully defended after a famous affray in Soho in 1955, said, "If you want something to write about, write about Rose Heilbron, she's the greatest lawyer in history."

Rose was the first woman to plead a case in the House of Lords, and in 1956 she became the first woman recorder appointed for Burnley. The journalists who crowded into Burnley Crown Court to watch her first case chose to focus on the way she fussed over her white starch neckbands, twisted her wedding ring and touched her crimson lipstick to test for smudging.

She sat as a judge at the Old Bailey in January 1972, and in October 1974 became only the second woman to be appointed to the High Court, in that role. In September 1975, she overruled doctors who wanted to sterilise an 11-year-old girl with Sotos syndrome, which made her physically advanced despite learning difficulties. It is also known as cerebral gigantism because of the distinctive head shape and size. That year, she also chaired the Home Secretary, Roy Jenkins' Advisory Group, which led to a change in the law of rape. In 1976, she was made an Honorary Fellow of Lady Margaret Hall, Oxford, where her daughter had received a degree.

In 1981 she presided over the longest murder trial at Lancaster

Crown Court, the so-called 'Mr Asia' case, when a handless and mutilated body was found in a flooded quarry in Lancashire. This was then Britain's most expensive case, the six-month trial of an international drug trafficker who was convicted of the grisly murder of an associate. Rose Heilbron recommended that he serve at least 20 years in prison. She also suggested that the defendant, Alexander Sinclair, pay £1m towards the prosecution costs, saying she had been told he was worth £25m, "give or take a million or two". In one of her last cases in 1987, she refused to allow an Oxford student to intervene in the decision by his former girl friend to have an abortion.

After becoming Treasurer at Gray's Inn in 1985, she said of her appointment, "The legal world does not discriminate by sex or race and this is possibly an example of it working rather well." Her hobbies included golf and walking, and she was a keen member of Soroptimist International, the worldwide organisation for women in management and professions, working to advance human rights and the status of women. She retired in 1988, aged 74, to pursue her interests in gardening, golf and music. Rose Heilbron died December 8, 2005. Her husband and daughter, Hilary Heilbron QC, survived her. 'The Telegraph' on the 12, December 2005 stated:

> Her qualities included a crystal-clear mind and a fine incisive voice. She was also a tremendous fighter and a prodigiously hard worker, willing to toil around the clock on difficult cases. Her advocacy was sometimes unorthodox but always eloquent. Her tenacity enabled her to dominate the courtroom, in spite of her quiet demeanour, which put some in mind of a housewife. At the height of her celebrity in the 1950s, the darkly handsome Rose Heilbron received requests from young men for photos of herself in her bathing costume, and an offer of marriage from a man in West Africa.
>
> Had she been a man, Rose Heilbron's appointment to the bench would almost certainly have come almost ten years sooner. Perhaps also because of her sex, she was not assigned to the Queen's Bench Division where her vast experience as a criminal practitioner could best have been put to use presiding over major criminal trials, but instead shunted into the Family

Division. She was a great success there, however, her warmth and common sense made her particularly outstanding in cases dealing with children.

In December 2005, BBC Radio 4 invited her former colleague Lord Hoosen, Judge Frances Kirkham and Judge Constance Briscoe to discuss how far women had really come in the judiciary. Each one of them spoke highly of Dame Rose Heilbron. 'The Times' in its obituary said of her:

There was nothing flamboyant about Rose Heilbron's style of questioning. In court cross-examining, she was precise, persuasive and direct. Her ability to seize on the salient facts and destroy her opponent's case made her renowned as a defence barrister, with successes in some of the most notable trials of the day.

There was then no other woman at the Bar of her stature, fulfilling a promise that singled her out from the time she first decided to take up the law as a profession and led eventually to her becoming a High Court judge. As such she won a reputation for careful erudition and compassion.

Chapter 2

*M*argaret *K*elly

*M*argaret was born on 24th June 1910, at the Rotunda Hospital in Parnell Street, Dublin, and christened Margaret Kelly. Her mother's maiden name was Margaret O'Brien, her father was James Kelly but there is some suggestion that her parents had not married. Some weeks after her birth a priest visited the family, which consisted of three sisters and their brother, who were living in O'Connell Street, Dublin. He suggested to the sisters that perhaps Mary, Margaret's eldest sister, whom he judged more suitable, should look after the baby for three months. The parents of the infant were about to go abroad and could not take the baby with them. She agreed, although life in the working class area of Dublin in 1910 was hard for Mary Murphy, a spinster, and the rest of her family, without having a newborn infant trust upon them. Caring for the child turned out to be for much longer than the original request. She was sickly and never knew her real parents.

In 1913 the infamous Dublin Lockout occurred bringing the

city to a stand-still, when most factories and places of employment shut out their workers during a strike called by Liverpool born Trade Union Leader, James Larkin. Many people found it hard to put food on the table at this time, so work for Mary Murphy, skilled as a dressmaker, was not always available. Mary was reduced to scrubbing floors and paid a neighbour to look after Bluebell, as the baby was then known. Life became no better for those living in Dublin and resulted in the Easter Rising of 1916. Margaret was then just a few months from her sixth birthday. The battle taking place in Dublin was the start of a long and bloody campaign that was to continue until 1922, which brought about the Irish Free State, comprising twenty-six counties of the thirty-two counties, the other six remaining in British hands.

The fighting on the streets and the economic situation convinced Mary Murphy she would be better off in Liverpool with Bluebell and her three other adopted children. Mary therefore turned her back on Dublin and headed for the ferry to join the many thousands of Irish people who had poured into the great port of Liverpool. She eventually settled in West Derby, which was a district where she had many relations on the outskirts of the town, away from most of the poverty and bad housing in 1916. Most working class houses in those days were lucky to have running water but had no access to hot water or bathrooms. Mary and Bluebell were able to avail themselves of the public washhouse and slipper baths where they could look forward to a nice hot bath once a week for a couple of coppers. ‿

Bluebell was straightaway enrolled into Leyfield Convent, a boarding school that took in a few children with limited means as day pupils. At the age of eight she enrolled into Madame Cummings' dancing school in Liverpool. It was a hard struggle for Mary Murphy to find the tram fares and the half crown a week for the dance school that would give Bluebell more than a better social standing as it was hoped to give her a future away from poverty. The school approved of her dancing and gave Bluebell a platform to entertain other pupils with displays of her dance routines.

At the age of 12, Bluebell took to caddying at the nearby

golf course used by the middle class, to help pay for her dancing lessons. She also started delivering such newspapers as the 'Daily Telegraph' and 'The Times' for her local newsagent and the sight of the middle class houses showed her that there was more to life than poverty. Bluebell would do any part-time job after school hours to help her Auntie Mary pay for the dancing lessons and, in time, her hard work paid off. To the delight of Mary Murphy, Bluebell was offered her first professional job, 'Babes in the Wood', a pantomime put on by a children's dancing troupe ran for three weeks in a theatre in the seaside resort at Newquay, Cornwall. Other dancing engagements came Bluebell's way with Madame Cummings' troupe, and the little Dublin girl had arrived.

The love and devotion of Mary Murphy was being rewarded and she had a right to be proud of herself and of Bluebell. Not only did the dancing help to strengthen her limbs but also she was soon the star pupil. The following year, Bluebell appeared in 'Sinbad the Sailor' at the Rotunda Theatre, Scotland Road in Liverpool. By the time Bluebell was fourteen she was looking for new horizons, the world of dance had consumed her and was to be her El Dorado. At the age of 14 she had left school to tour Scotland with a cabaret troupe, the Hot Jocks.

Her first experience of life on the road – 'Bluebell'
(second on left with the Hot Jocks)

Bluebell soon came to the attention of impresario Alfred Jackson, who signed her up as a dancer in Berlin. Every day she would join the Jackson Girls' crocodile, walking in pairs to the Scala theatre. The sight of the girls snaking through the streets provided good publicity. Bluebell joined the Jackson Girls at the Scala, Berlin, and at 19 was taken on as chorus line holiday cover at Folies Bergère, in Paris.

Her self-discipline caused the Folies management to ask her to form an in-house dance troupe and she soon fell in love with the city. Two years later Jackson invited her to form her own troupe and the Les Blue Bell's Girls were born. But a disagreement caused Margaret to move her dance troupe successfully to the Paramount Cinema, performing between films. Patching up differences, she formed a second troupe for the Follies. She kept a gimlet eye on her protégés at the Folies Bergère and, later, the Lido in Paris. Everything from breaking dress codes to curfews would earn a swift rebuke from Margaret and, with good reason, she would say, "Chorus girls had a bad reputation when I started. Everyone thought they went into dancing as a means to after-show activities. I wasn't having any of that and I insisted on them being absolutely correct". Sharon Wright, in the 'Daily Express', Thursday, September 16 2004, wrote:

> The courage of 'Miss Bluebell' Margaret Kelly, who has died this week, was the founder of a legendary dance troupe and during the war laughed in the face of Nazi terror. Whether breaking the mould with her Amazonian dancers clad in feathers and sequins or standing up to the Gestapo in occupied Paris, she was one of a kind. Better known as the legendary Miss Bluebell, she saw herself as a second mother to her crème-de-la-crème chorus girls – though they might have seen it differently. She was undoubtedly loved, according to her biographer, George Perry, but 'in the way one would love a strict colonel, someone you were glad to have on your side if you went into battle'.
>
> Indeed Miss Bluebell or simply Miss died this week after making more of an impact on Europe than many generals. She brought glamour to a captivated Paris and built a fortune

with her dancers, the Bluebell Girls. She was still capable of surprising Michael Parkinson with an impromptu high kick well into her 70s and had celebrities paying her court for more than half a century. But away from the theatre she showed her true mettle in the dark days of Nazi occupation of Paris, then braving the Gestapo to hide her Jewish husband.

The payoff was big wages, high-octane glamour, celebrity fans and the kudos of belonging to the dancing elite. Thanks to Miss Bluebell it was, everyone agreed, the best job a girl could get. Margaret was a sickly baby. It was a doctor who first looked into her piercing blue eyes and called her "my little Bluebell", while another sealed her fate by recommending therapeutic dancing. During the five years there she joined the artistic milieu of the late twenties that included Marlene Dietrich and Christopher Isherwood. But, in 1930, there were already darker forces gathering in Germany. "She thought British girls were better then French girls," says Perry. "She used British girls who were classically trained but too tall for the ballet."

She stopped dancing herself, growing famous in her own right as a formidable management talent, with her shows quickly becoming fashionable entertainment. She was also falling in love, with Marcel Leibovici, a Jewish Romanian pianist who worked with her at the Folies Bergère. They were married in Paris in 1939. Her devotion to her husband proved to be every bit as steely as her devotion to her girls, almost costing her her life. But not once did she knuckle down to the Nazi demands.

However, when the Germans invaded in 1940 the couple fled to Bordeaux in the hope of escaping to Britain. But they had left it too late and had to return to Paris where Bluebell was arrested for holding a British passport, and interned at Besancon. Far from crumbling, Bluebell who was pregnant quickly took charge of her fellow prisoners and raised morale by refusing to obey her captors. When ordered to scrub floors she declared: "I don't do that kind of thing at home so I am not going to do it here."

Meanwhile Marcel was persuading the Irish ambassador to

argue for her release as an Irish national. After three months, Bluebell was released. By then, it was clear that Jewish Marcel was in most danger. He fled but he was caught and sent to camp in the Pyrenees. He escaped back to Paris and went into hiding, spending two years in an attic in a building opposite the police station. After the war, they discovered the landlady was an informant and it was only the fact that Bluebell unwittingly paid her 10 francs more than the Nazis that saved his life.

It was a terrifying time for Bluebell. She would load up with supplies for Marcel and cycle through the occupied streets. She was walking a tight-rope but never lost her nerve, even when hauled in by the Gestapo for interrogation. A furious SS officer barked "We want to know where your husband is." "So do I!" was her retort. Despite her clutch of close calls, when the Germans inevitably asked her to entertain the troops she refused, appealing to their code of honour by claiming to have relatives in the British army. And even as the allied troops drew near in 1944, she almost suffered an eleventh-hour calamity. Not content with making it so far, she sent off to demand compensation from the Germans who had removed the tyres from Marcel's car. On her way back she was caught in a firefight between German troops and the French Resistance. As the bullets whizzed around, she fell off her bicycle and lay with one famous leg suspended in the air, too terrified to move it in case she caught the attention of a marksman. Finally, a young German with a machine gun approached her.

"You can bloody well hop it," she said, and watched as he did. Then, in 1961, Marcel was killed in a car crash. Bluebell was devastated. Left with four young children, Patrick, Francis, Florence, Jean-Paul, and a business to run, she managed to pull herself together and take over Marcel's role. By the Seventies, she was the centre of an empire, with troupes stretching from Hong Kong to Las Vegas. She lived in a penthouse and travelled the world. In 1971, the Bluebells went topless. And the morally upstanding Miss Bluebell saw nothing insalubrious in that. "There's no sex involved," she said. "It's just an extension of parading beautiful bodies, combined with high class-dance. One expects that in a top class show."

At the age of 70, she was in the MGM Grand Hotel in Las

Vegas when a fireball from the kitchen tore across the casino. Bluebell was trapped in her room with 30 other people praying for rescue. When one lit a cigarette she snapped: "Put that out, there's enough smoke in here!" More than 80 people died but Bluebell emerged, as ever unscathed. She finally officially retired when she was approaching 80, but remained spry and mischievous enough to punctuate her appearance on the Michael Parkinson show by standing up and performing the high-kick. It was her party trick and she talked proudly of the time she met John and Norma Major. "They asked if I was still in shape," she recalled. "I gave them a high kick to prove it."

Throughout her extraordinary career, she was a true celebrity. Everyone from Brigitte Bardot, Elizabeth Taylor and Richard Burton to Sacha Distel joined her at her table at the Lido. She met the Pope, and was awarded the OBE. She took French citizenship in 1948 and received the Legion of Honour and the Legion of Merit and was made a Chevalier des Arts et Lettres. In 1986 her life was turned into the BBC drama 'Bluebell', where Carolyn Pickle played her. Her later years were overshadowed by infighting among her three surviving children over her estate (Jean-Paul died in 1996) but she had plenty of memories in which to take refuge. "She was one of the most remarkable women of the 20th century," says George Perry, who knew her well while writing her 1986 biography. "She was a strong determined, unstoppable character, a legend. I found her inspiring," and, as the curtain finally closed on the life of the indomitable Miss Bluebell, he is not alone. 'The Liverpool Daily Post', Thursday, September 16 2004, paid a fitting tribute to Margaret in its obituary:

> Her life was the stuff of those popular romances that used the pre-World War 1, Liverpool, as the colourful background for a poor but feisty girl to get on against overwhelming odds. She was the little Irish orphan baby, sickly and weak, about whom a kindly doctor said: "If I was your mother with those eyes, I should call you Bluebell." And so a legend was born, Margaret Kelly, who has died, aged 94, gravitated to Paris and in 1932 founded one of the most famous dance troupes ever, the Bluebell Girls. Their

average 5ft 11 height made them four inches taller than Margaret herself. She didn't think her childhood at Deysbrook Lane, West Derby, was deprived, saying: "I was always well dressed and had enough jam butties to eat."

She owned the Bluebell Girls in Las Vegas and Reno, the Bluebell Nude Dances ("nothing sleazy or pornographic" she said). She was married to Jewish Romanian pianist, Marcel Leibovici, she hid him for two years during the Nazi occupation of Paris, after the Irish Ambassador saved her from internment. Three children of their children survive her.

Margaret Fox, The New York Times, 2005 wrote:

Margaret Kelly, a proper Irishwoman better known as Miss Bluebell who founded the Bluebell Girls, the long-stemmed, high-kicking, slightly clad troupe considered the most glamorous chorus line in Paris and perhaps the world, died in her sleep on Sept. 11 at her home in Paris, her son Patrick Leibovici said. She was 94. Founded in 1932, the Bluebell Girls are one of the last remaining companies to dance the traditional 'can-can', with its flying kicks and punishing splits. They are still the featured act at the Lido, on the Champs-Élysées, performing in glittering clouds of sequins, ostrich feathers, voluminous headgear and not a great deal else. To generations of showgirls -- she is said to have trained 14,000 -- Miss Kelly was talent scout, taskmaster, chaperon, mother confessor and dispenser of tea. Until her retirement at 79, she supervised the Bluebells' every performance (two shows a day, seven days a week) with military precision, while ferociously guarding their virtue from a stream of stage-door Lotharios.

The troupe toured internationally and had resident companies in Reno, Nevada, and Las Vegas, where a colony of retired Bluebells still live. Bluebell told The Los Angeles Times in 1985, when referring to her dances, "They must have long legs, be at least 5-foot-10, with high, well-formed derrières, firm breasts, but not too large because, since the demise of the brassiere, dangling, voluminous breasts appear unpleasant, anti-aesthetic." Her life was the subject of a BBC mini-series, "Bluebell" in 1986, but Bluebell complained that the film's eight hours could scarcely begin to tell her story. She danced her way across the cabaret stages of Europe as a teenager; worked with Maurice Chevalier, Josephine Baker and Edith Piaf, was interned during World War II, saved her husband from the Nazis, raised four children, could still dance the can-can in her 60's, smoked a pack of cigarettes every day of her adult life, and was awarded the French Legion of Honour and the order of the British Empire.

Chapter 3

*M*argaret *S*imey

*M*argaret was born with the surname Todd in Glasgow in 1906, into a comfortable middle-class Presbyterian family. Margaret's family moved to London when she was quite young and she was educated at St Paul's Girls' School, West London, where she came into contact with Diana, a fellow pupil and daughter of Winston Churchill. Margaret moved to Liverpool at the age of 18, when her father became principal of the College of Commerce in Tithebarn Street. It was the start of a lifelong love affair with the city, and particularly its working class. She became the first female graduate in Social Science from Liverpool University in 1928 and it was at a University folk dance that she met the young Tom Simey and they married in 1935.

Tom Simey was the chairman of the Merseyside Refuge Committee during the 1930s. Because of the Anti-Semitic Movement in Germany, the Simeys gave a home to eight German Jewish refuges. Thomas Simey became Professor of

Social Science in 1939 and in 1965 was made a Life Peer. Together they spent most of the war years in the Caribbean as part of a small team of experts on social and economic development. This experience, and their other international interests, gave them both a deep respect for the Afro-Caribbean and Chinese communities in the hinterland of the Liverpool docks.

From the mid-1940s, Margaret became involved in many of the fields of voluntary service, which have flourished on Merseyside for more than a century. She traced the origins of this tradition in Charitable Effort In Liverpool in 1951. Later, in 1960 she and her husband wrote their definitive study of Charles Booth, who first recognised the limitations of charity giving throughout the country. Margaret Simey participated vigorously in these developments. As a Labour city councillor for Granby Ward from 1963, she demonstrated both the depth of her local knowledge and her impatience with many of the structures of local government. She realised that, despite all the community institutions, poor people were losing out further, as Liverpool went deeper into economic decline.

In the immediate post war period and until the 1970s, Toxteth was an area rich in voluntary organisations that signified, but also often bridged, many cultural and religious divides. It was here that the principles of community development were tested, neighbourhood projects proliferated and, eventually, community councils were set up to give local people a chance to voice their views, to respond to each other's needs and, increasingly, to put pressure on the city council, which often seemed remote and authoritarian, no matter what party was in power.

She became a national figure from the mid-1970s, through her election as a member, and later Chairman, of the Merseyside Police Authority, which led her to question the behaviour of the police and the role of the Chief Constable, Sir Kenneth Oxford, before and after the 1981 disturbances in Toxteth. She also came into conflict with Margaret Thatcher and Michael Heseltine.

When local government was reorganised in 1974, Margaret was elected to the Merseyside County Council, and in 1981 became Chairman of the Police Authority. In Liverpool, relations between the police and local neighbourhoods were often fragile, especially among the increasingly segregated black communities, resulting in the eventual breakdown of relations. She said of those local people involved in the confrontation with the police that "they would be apathetic fools if they didn't protest."

Race, unemployment and the police service occupied much of her time on Merseyside's Police Committee. Margaret came to national prominence during the Toxteth riots of 1981, (much to Margaret Thatcher's annoyance). Margaret was also engaged in long tussles with the Chief Constable, Kenneth Oxford.

She found it hard to bear the subsequent abuse directed at her by much of the media. There was a tense period as she and her elected colleagues sought to establish the accountability of the police and the role and responsibility of the Chief Constable. In 1986 the Merseyside County Council was abolished and she was succeeded as a local city councillor and to her great delight, by a young black woman. Margaret continued as an informal counsellor, working with family groups, youth clubs, voluntary organisations and ecumenical enterprises. She was also much sought after as a public speaker throughout the country.

For more than 60 years she was a social activist. Margaret Simey became one of the best known local figures, tall and purposeful, as she urgently strode the city streets. She was fearless for herself and indomitable in her support of local people, urging them to speak and act for themselves and identifed with them in good times and bad. Her style and the strength of her convictions were such that, to many in authority and in the media, she invited contention and misunderstanding. "I am," she would say, "a dogged woman. I never condoned violence but I warned of it. I saw people being neglected and disenfranchised, a community being subjected to dependence".

Margaret could sometimes appear austere and intimidating. Her quiet, cultured Scottish voice could be forthright and vigorous in public advocacy. She recognised that her "habitual irony" was offensive to many. Yet she remained gracious and generous in her personal relationships and was able to elicit a warm, individual response from people of all ages. In old age she was awarded an honorary doctorate of the University of Liverpool for her services to the community. In her eighties she was an honorary Senior Fellow of the University, still actively learning, teaching, writing and speaking, though when she was offered the freedom of the city, she turned it down flat.

It was Harold Wilson who had made Margaret's husband a life peer, but she preferred to be known simply as Margaret Simey. It is this name that was included in 'Who's Who', and which takes its place among a group of exceptional women including Kitty Wilkinson, Josephine Butler, Eleanor Rathbone and Dorothy Keeling, whose service to the city and its people covered more than a century, and resounded far beyond Merseyside.

"I am my own visual aid", wrote Margaret in her last published book, which came out when she was 90. 'The Disinherited Society' was subtitled 'A Personal View of Social Responsibility in Liverpool During the Twentieth Century'. The long life of Margaret Simey, who died in hospital aged 98, was dedicated to the people of Liverpool and especially to Toxteth and similar inner-city neighbourhoods.

Margaret produced a steady flow of books from 'Charles Booth' (1960), a life of a the social researcher and anti poverty-campaigner, written with her husband, to 'Government by Consent' (1985), exploring the principal and practice of accountability in local government, 'Democracy Rediscovered', a study of philanthropic effort in nineteenth-century Liverpool (1992) and 'The Disinherited Society' (1960). There were also countless papers, articles, lectures and reviews. 'From Rhetoric to Reality, life and work of Frederick D'Aeth', the founding lecturer in Social Science at Liverpool University, was published in March 2005.

Chapter 4

Ethel Austin

We live in an age of celebrities, but in many cases they are people who do not appear to have contributed much to society. They are there, most of the time at the switch of the television button or on the front page of our newspapers. However, just like a fallen leaf from a tree, they are soon blown away in the passage of time.

When the name of Ethel Austin first appeared in the minds of the general public, it had taken many years of hard work for this to happen. She was a family woman who had a dream that would take her away from the mundane chores of the household in the 1930s. It was a time of great poverty in many towns and cities, a time when many businesses collapsed or went into receivership. Liverpool suffered greatly during this period. The lifeblood of the port had almost dried up when many of the ships that traded with the rest of the world were laid up. People were grateful to earn a few shillings for half a day's work on the docks and a chance to feed their families. There was no welfare state, no 'National Health Service' and people needed paying.

Ethel Laycock was born on the 8th March 1900, the middle child of nine. The family lived in Cockburn Street in the Dingle district of Liverpool, but later moved to nearby Grafton Street. This house was very tall and from the upstairs windows there was an extensive view of the river, the docks and the overhead railway, which ran alongside the dock road. This was the first electrically powered overhead railway in the world. Sadly, it had to be demolished in 1957 because the company could not afford the two million pounds needed for repairs. Not far from them was the Cast Iron Shore where her six brothers used to play.

Ethel with her mother, grandfather and five of her brothers

Ethel's father, Edwin, was a butcher and also worked as a cooper, making barrels. When no other work was available, he sometimes worked on the docks. The family was respectable but poor and Ethel's mother, Mary Ann, had high standards. They brought up their children to be honest and hard-working, and were proud of the fact that they reared nine children, as infant mortality was high. Mary Ann's father and brother lived with them after the death of her mother, as well as any other members of her large family who needed a temporary home.

The only running water in the house came from the cold water tap over the sink in the large scullery, and in the corner stood a boiler which had to be filled from the tap. There was a huge mangle in the middle of the room and a tin bath hung on the wall. Their outside toilet was in the corner of the backyard. The semi-basement kitchen was at the front of the house and above it was the sitting room. This room was reserved for special occasions, as the family usually gathered in the kitchen, which was warmed by the kitchen range.

Ethel had a happy childhood, although living conditions seem very harsh viewed from the 21st century, and her parents were strict. She was expected to help her mother by looking after her four younger brothers, darning their socks, which was a never-ending task, and scrubbing floors. She had a good, basic education at school and when she left at the age of 14, she started work as a shop assistant. Ethel was very well suited to the job as she had a friendly personality and enjoyed her contact with customers.

At the age of 19 she began to rebel against the strict discipline of her parents and was punished by having to leave the job she loved, to work in a paper factory, which was extremely boring. At the time, she was going out with George Austin, whom she had known for quite a while. Their first meeting was on Sefton Park lake, when she was boating with her friends and he was in another boat with his friends.

George was 22 years old and had served in the First World War from 1914 to 1918. Although only 16 when the war started, he had given his age as 18 and joined up with the Liverpool Pals. He spent the war years living in the trenches in Belgium which was then known as Flanders, enduring great hardships and constant danger. He had been a clever boy at school, helping to teach boys who were lagging behind, but there was no opportunity for him to have further education, so after leaving the army, he worked as a tram driver with the Liverpool Corporation. He was an engaging young man, who fell in love with Ethel and swept her off her feet.

George Austin

George and Ethel wanted to get married, but Ethel was only just 20 years old and did not have her parents' permission, so she gave her age as 22 when they were married in a register office on the 22nd May 1920, the only other people present being two friends. They went back to their own homes, but Ethel's courage failed her and she kept her marriage secret.

Some months later during an argument, her mother told her that when she got married she could do as she liked, but until then she had to obey her parents. Ethel's response was "I am married and I will do as I like." When her mother recovered from the shock of this revelation, she insisted that there must be a public ceremony to prove that she was married and preserve her good name.

The second wedding took place in October after which Ethel and George set up home together. The following September their son Ronald was born. Daughter Lesley was born in 1925, and a second daughter Glenys in 1928. Their younger son, Graeme, made his appearance much later in 1938. In February 1936, Lesley died in hospital, losing her brave battle against septicaemia the day after her 11th birthday. This was a great loss for the family and Ethel felt the pain of her death for the rest of her life.

When an insurance policy matured in 1934, they had £50 to spend. They discussed buying new furniture, which they needed, but Ethel wanted to open a flower shop. George was more practical. Times were hard and there would not be much money available for the luxury of buying flowers. Ethel was very good at knitting which they thought could be used to advantage, so after much discussion, they decided to open a wool shop.

They found a tiny shop, converted from the front room of a terraced house, which they rented, and bought a small stock of wool, patterns and knitting needles. There were so many bare shelves that they went looking for empty boxes to fill them. Their son Ronald, aged 13, was sent out to deliver leaflets to neighbouring houses bearing the message "Bring your knitting problems to Ethel Austin at 2a Bishop Road". They wanted to call the shop 'Austins', but there was an objection as the name was already in use, so they decided to use Ethel's name.

The venture was a success, mainly because any profits were used to buy more stock and improve the shop, while they lived on George's wages as a tram driver. Ethel could show her neighbours how to follow complicated instructions in the pattern books and pick up dropped stitches; she loved company and was happy chatting to customers as she helped them with their knitting. When they could not afford to buy the full amount of wool needed to complete a garment, they would buy one ounce at a time and the rest was put away for them. Ethel started to give credit, but some people let her down and she had to stop when George, who took care of the finances, said that they could not afford it.

Ethel Austin's first shop 1934.
2A Bishop Road, Anfield, Liverpool

George had acquired a smoking habit while serving as a soldier in the First World War, but whenever money was required to buy clothes or shoes for the children or for an extra expense, he would give up cigarettes so that they could afford to pay for them without borrowing. They had never been in debt but once they were in business, they were not always able to pay bills right away. This would worry Ethel, but George reassured her that all would be well and would say "As long as the kids are alright there's nothing to worry about". Ethel was quite embarrassed to read in their daughter's school exercise book a description of her mother which included the words "My mother doesn't worry about the money she owes".

Although ultimately successful, there were times when the business could have failed without George's careful management. He became adept at totting up a list of sales on a sheet of foolscap paper with never a mistake, although the figures would be in pounds, shillings, pence, halfpennies and farthings and this was without a calculator. He had no knowledge of book keeping, but learned as he went along.

After two years in the little shop they were able to expand their business and opened a shop in Walton Village which had accommodation for the family behind and above the shop premises. This was a practical and convenient move, but there was no garden. Ethel was very sad to leave behind the garden she had enjoyed at her council house. The shop was large enough to stock ladies' underwear, hosiery, baby linen, etc as well as wool, and was now what was known as a 'draper's shop' instead of a 'wool shop'. Only one year later, Ethel and George opened another shop in Breck Road and closed the tiny shop in Bishop Road. Their son, Ronald, who had been working in the Co-op since leaving school, joined them when he was 17 and helped to run the business, which was now thriving.

In the summer of 1938 there was a phone call from a youth hostel in North Wales. Ronald, who was rock-climbing in the area, was suffering from acute abdominal pain, nausea and vomiting. He was taken to hospital and diagnosed with Bright's Disease, a severe kidney infection. Having already lost a daughter two years earlier, his parents were very anxious, but Ronald recovered enough to be taken home where he was put on a strict diet and made a good recovery.

They were doing well and were able to buy their first car: the family moved to a four bedroom detached house in 1939. During the war they continued to be successful, but it was more difficult. Everything was in short supply and customers were limited as to how much they could spend by rationing. The allowance for all clothing was 66 coupons per person, enough to buy one complete outfit a year. People got used to recycling instead of buying new. Dishcloth cotton could be used instead of wool and it did not need coupons, so George would chase up supplies as often as he could. He left his job with Liverpool Corporation and joined the Home Guard. They opened two more shops, one in Walton Breck Road in 1945 and the other in Church Road, Litherland, in 1947.

Ronald – RAF Days

Their son, Ronald served in the RAF during the war and wanted to fly Spitfires. He was disappointed when he was sent to Canada to train other pilots, but did enjoy his time there. Canadians were very hospitable and he was often invited to visit people in their homes. Ethel wanted to do the same for other young servicemen who were far from home, on leave in England.

She contacted the British Council who arranged for fifteen young men from allied countries to stay in her home at various times during the war, some of them more than once. One of her Canadian guests, who stayed with the family several times, kept in touch and returned to visit with his wife many years later.

Ronald returned to England after the war intending to stay in the RAF, but his future wife, Pat, persuaded him to leave, because she thought flying was too dangerous. His parents were delighted to welcome him back to work with them and together they opened a large shop in Old Swan, Liverpool, in 1948. Ronald was appointed managing director in 1949 and George continued to work in the business until he retired at the age of 75. Ethel gradually bowed out, leaving further development to her husband and son. She did not work again until the 1960s when she helped other volunteers to run a small shop serving patients and visitors in the Liverpool Royal Infirmary.

In July 1947 George wrote in his journal, "We are all blessed with something or other. I am well blessed with a determined wife, so when she suggested that we should motor across France for our holiday, I knew that nothing short of a war would stop us." Ethel and George with Glenys and Graeme drove to Canterbury, where they would spend the night in a hotel before crossing to France with their car the following day. On their arrival at the hotel, George discovered with horror that the briefcase containing their passports and money was missing. It was where he had left it - by the front door of their house ready to pick up on leaving. As it happened, they left by the side door, leaving Ronald to lock up. He noticed the briefcase by the door after they had gone, rang the hotel to leave a message, and set off after them. It was a great relief to all the family, but particularly to George, when Ronald arrived at the hotel carrying the briefcase.

Graeme, George, Glenys and Ethel. South of France 1947

After the family arrived in France, they drove to Paris and continued south, stopping at small hotels on the way until they reached Marseille. They had been invited to stay with a family whose son had been their guest at Christmas. The family made them very welcome, taking them to Nice and Monte Carlo and visiting other resorts on the Riviera. Ethel wanted to return their hospitality, so she invited them all to come and stay England. In order to accommodate their extended family members, she rented an old manor house near Pwhelli in Wales where her family welcomed them. They all had a wonderful time in spite of cold and wet weather and George had to admit that it had been a good idea.

Other family holidays in France were spent visiting friends and staying in hotels. Ethel enjoyed many holidays abroad as long as she was fit to travel. When she was older and travelling became more difficult, she found that cruise ships suited her needs. One of her trips was a Round the World Cruise, so she was able to see many places which would otherwise have been beyond her reach.

When Ethel was a child, her father took her to visit a large, imposing house with a beautiful garden: since then it had always been her ambition to live in such a house and she found one in Birkenhead. When she persuaded George to go with her to view it she met with strong resistance but, as usual, she eventually won him over and they moved there in 1955. More furniture was needed, so she made visits to auction rooms, buying large pieces of furniture and pictures and ornaments for the house. Her daughter lived in a separate part of the house with her husband, who worked in the business, and their two daughters. Ronald had one daughter and Graeme had two daughters, completing the family which would gather together at Ethel's home on special occasions.

The first staff party of the Ethel Austin Company was a small affair held in January 1948 at Reece's Restaurant, which was attended by the family and the staff of 4 shops. This became an annual event at which Ethel would enjoy talking to the staff members. In 1984 the Golden Anniversary of the Company was celebrated by the family with the staff from 65 shops at the Adelphi Hotel in Liverpool. Ethel died at home in 1989 and when the company was sold in 2002, there were more than 200 shops in all parts of the country proudly displaying her name.

It was Ethel's wish that her funeral should be a quiet, family affair and so it was. However, a Memorial Service to celebrate her life was held later. All the shops closed for the day and many of the staff attended as well as family friends. A bed of beautiful pink 'Ethel Austin' roses was planted in Ness Botanic Gardens on the Wirral, a fitting tribute to a lady who loved flowers.

*Ethel with husband George
1920*

*Ethel and George with two
of their children*

*Ethel and two neighbours
1921*

*Ethel and Lesley,
New Brighton 1926*

Ethel with Ronald, Lesley and baby Glenys 1928

Ethel's parents at the wedding of their eldest grandson 1938

*Ethel, Lesley and Glenys
in the garden of their council house 1929*

Ethel's mum with Ronald, Ethel and Glenys

Ethel and Ronald 1938

George, Ethel, Glenys and Graeme 1943

Glenys and Ethel with a French friend 1948

Ronald, Ethel and George 1952

Ethel's home in Birkenhead 1955-1989

Ethel pictured in 1983

Chapter 5

$\mathscr{L}$izzie $\mathscr{C}$hristian

*F*or many centuries street traders have brought colour and communication to the streets of our land, and we see it still in the small towns around the country but there are times when they are not always welcome because they are deemed to be in the way of the established business on the high street. Liverpool in many respects was built on street trade, as items from the many ships that entered the port could be sold straight from the dockside. Fishmongers, fruit and vegetable stalls together with the colourful flower sellers have been an everyday occurrence as far back to the time of King John when he entered Liverpool in 1207.

Lizzie Christian was a legend in Liverpool for more than sixty years, selling flowers from her pitch in the city centre. She was there from 9 in the morning until she made her way home at 6 in the evening, winter and summer, six days a week, and on Sundays she would be found outside the old Newsham General Hospital, Belmont Road, Liverpool. She was born in

1898, in Hawke Street, the Brownlow Hill area of the town, to docker, James Hawker and Rebecca Paroni. The eldest of twelve children, she married at 20, and brought up seven children. Lizzie supported her family by scrubbing steps, and by selling flowers from a big basket, to what she called "posh" people in the suburbs of south Liverpool, then later from her famous flower stall outside Central Station, and Clayton Square after she was moved on due to the reorganisation of the area.

She was a tiny woman, with her trademark headscarf, boots and often torn coat, working in rain, hail, snow or sun. She knew everyone from judges to "working girls", from M.P.'s like Bessie Braddock to local villains, as well as most of the stars and they all knew her. She was no stranger to controversy, having to move from one site to another; her son Jack worked alongside her for many years, and the Christian family, selling fruit and vegetables, is still very much part of Liverpool city life. Speaking on Radio Merseyside Lizzie's son Jack said:

"She could sit selling flowers outside Central Station all day on her own, and no harm would come to her". Everybody that came into contact with her respected Lizzie, and she was never bothered by any undesirables who might be on the lookout to relieve some innocent soul of their belongings.

Lizzie and her flower stall were eventually moved from the site outside Central Station where she had become a legend. People expected to see Lizzie as they left the station to do their shopping and the business people would look forward to buying an apple or orange from her to have with their lunch. She and her flowers could bring a bright smile from her customers or passers by on a dark winter's morning.

Lizzie was still working at the age of seventy-five, and like most things in life, nothing stays the same. Lizzie was moved to another pitch outside St. Johns Precinct, she settled into her new venue only to be told she would have to move again a few years later. She never had the financial muscle to fight her corner, her handcart and blooming flowers finished up in Casey Street just across the road from her most famous pitch, Central Station, then moved on again to Clayton Square, where she stayed until she retired through ill health.

The only enjoyment that she enjoyed outside her home, was the Shakespeare Theatre in Camden Street, Liverpool. Jean, her daughter-law, tells the story about Lizzie arriving home, and telling the family that a cowboy paid for a taxi to take her home when she finished work. The cowboy turned out to be P. J. Proby, the American singer who was appearing at the 'Wooky Hollow' theatre. He invited Lizzie and other members of her family to have dinner with him there after taking her backstage to meet the other performers.

Lizzie died in 1977 and the stars of stage and screen paid their respects to a woman who was colourful and bright as the flowers she sold. The family tell the story about the funeral being a private family affair, and a request that no flowers be sent. However this did not stop Bessie Braddock turning up with flowers for the little woman for whom she had great respect. David Charters of The Liverpool Daily Post, wrote:

There wasn't a silver spoon to sweeten life for Lizzie Christian, one of 12 children born to the docker James Hawker and his Italian wife, Rebecca Paroni. But what a face our Lizzie had, creased over the flowers and fruit on her barrow. She was a Victorian story made flesh, made blood and made courage. On the coldest days, she could be heard calling the price of apples and oranges from her pitch on Casey Street. When times were tougher than usual, she scrubbed steps to supplement her income. In all this time, she never smoked or drank or saw a "moving picture show". But she had been married to "handsome" Jack Christian, a soldier, who left her with seven children. Lizzie supported them all and their children loved her as well. Yes, you can talk of the Mona Lisa with her enigmatic smile and you can stroll the portrait galleries of the world. But you will never see a face like that on our Lizzie Christian, staring through the fog of another age. She is forever Liverpool.

Chapter 6

Elizabeth Margaret Braddock

*E*lizabeth Margaret Bamber, better known as Bessie, was born in Zante Street, Liverpool, on September 24, 1899, and known through out her life as Bessie. Her parents were Mary and Hugh Bamber and at an early age she was introduced to her family struggle to improve the lot of the lower economic classes. Her mother was the national organiser of the 'National Union of Distributive and Allied Workers' and was a Labour party worker. Her father was an active Liverpool Socialist and Bessie had a good working class background as he started work at the age of 14 in 1883, and retired after 53 years from Tinling and Co, printers in Victoria Street, Liverpool.

Bessie attended school until she was fifteen, and went to work as an assistant in the Liverpool Co-operative Society. During World War I, she belonged to pacifist groups and in the post-war years participated in unemployment demonstrations in Liverpool and became an active trade unionist and political worker.

Bessie Braddock claimed she was "born to the Socialist movement". At the age of 21, Bessie was in charge of an unemployment committee in the city. She later became the first woman President of the Liverpool Trades Council and Labour Party, and was a member of Labour's national executive committee. Bessie once likened the House of Commons, with its doors leading to the division lobby, to a comedy show, and insisted that the "soulless ritual" was in need of reform.

In 1922 she married John Braddock and in the early 1920s was for a short time a member of the Communist Party, resigning when she felt she was denied the right of independent thought and expression. In 1955 she stated: "The Communist party is rotten through and through". It was reported that she later also made a statement to the effect: "Don't worry, these Communists and neo-Communists won't get me out of Parliament." In 1930 Bessie was elected to the Liverpool City Council as Labour member for St. Ann's Ward; her husband John Braddock, was also a member of the City Council.

She first entered Parliament in 1945, when she won the Exchange Division for Labour with a majority of just 665. Five years later that had increased to more than 5,000 and it continued to increase. When elected to Westminster, Bessie was a housewife of 46. She led a campaign for improvement of housing. On several occasions she referred to the fleas, bugs and rats that infested the slums of Liverpool and promised: "To agitate and kick up a row until we get rid of these evils and I don't care whose houses we take." In her first year in Parliament 1945 she said of the slums, "Even if they're Lord Derby's or the Earl of Stamford's when working-class people are living like herrings in a tin."

City Council meetings were often stormy and Bessy earned a reputation for staging determined verbal fights. From 1955 she was an Alderman of the Council. It was said she was a vigilant guardian in the House of Commons, in the interests of British housewives. 'Battling' Bessie, as she was often called, never lost an election in the twenty-seven years of her political career. She was foe of both Conservative and Communist parties and a caustic critic of the Bevanite faction of the Labour party. Following her election to the House of

Commons, she was instrumental in ending the National Dock Strike of 1945. She served on the Liverpool City Council from 1930 and was widely loved in the city for her vigorous efforts to eliminate the slums that so many people had to endure, and replace them with better housing. Throughout her career she fought in the interests of the elderly and the poor.

Another aspect of her concern with community problems was her work for hospitals and maternity and child welfare. As Chairman of the Liverpool Maternity and Child Welfare Committee, she directed the founding of modern centres to carry out its activities. She was a member of the Assistance Board, Court of Referees and the Pensions Appeal Tribunal. Bessie Braddock helped to establish about ten old-age homes in Liverpool and assisted Liverpudlian pugilists in setting up their own gymnasium. She sponsored a number of Nigerian boxers to come to Liverpool, and one of them referred to her as his 'English mother'. During World War II, in addition to her other activities, she was a full-time worker in the ambulance service. She became deputy divisional ambulance officer of her local division, drove an ambulance during the blitz, and instructed other drivers, but also had to take orders herself from the senior divisional officer.

The Exchange Division of Liverpool Labour Party elected Mrs. Elizabeth Margaret Braddock to represent them during the election of 1945 as a Member of Parliament. Her opponent was Colonel Sir John Shute, whom she defeated by a majority of 665 votes and until her victory, the 'Exchange Division' was regarded as a Tory stronghold. In her first year in Parliament Bessie Braddock helped to end a five-week national dock strike. The Merseyside dockers had refused to return to work until their claims were considered and George Isaacs, Minister of Labour and National Service, promised to negotiate within twenty-four hours after the resumption of work, but not before. On November 2 1945, Bessie spoke on the floor of the Commons and related how she had been asked by them to intervene in the strike. She told of how she had spoken to the Minister and of her talks with the national strike committees. This resulted in the men agreeing to return to work under a thirty-day truce. "This statement of mine," she said, "is the order for the men to resume work on Monday morning." In 1947 Betty wrote:

> Benefits are to be derived from a free exchange of goods between Great Britain and her colonies. If freely negotiated trade agreements between free peoples as a means of exchanging the finished products of our factories for the raw materials and food of other lands are not to be substituted for the swashbuckling domination that has held the Empire together for so long, then let us hand over the fruits of our victory at the polls to the die-hard Tories, who have known so long and practised so assiduously the policy of government by force in all parts of the Empire.

In 1947 she sued the proprietor of the Bolton (Lancashire) Evening News, claiming that in the May 1 1947 issue of the newspaper it was "wrongly alleged that she had danced a jig" and "sat in Winston Churchill's seat" the night the Bill nationalizing the trucking industry was passed. The defendant, Tillotson Newspapers Ltd., denied that the "words of the article were defamatory and pleaded that they were true in substance and fact." Witnesses testified at the trial that she had actually performed the acts attributed to her in the article. Mrs. Braddock lost the case, and judgment with costs was awarded to Tillotson Newspapers. Speaking in 1968 she deplored the fact that out of 630 MPs, only 26 were women. However she said that although few in numbers, they had managed to make their presence felt.

Following another of her determined efforts for which she was known in the House of Commons, she was ordered out of the House and suspended from attendance for five sessions on March 27 1952. She had insisted upon an opportunity to speak in a debate on the unemployment crisis in the textile industry. After refusing to be seated, and repeated requests by the Deputy Speaker, the House voted 127 to 67 to suspend her.

When the Members presented Sir Winston Churchill with a commemorative volume on the occasion of his eightieth birthday in 1954, Mrs. Braddock and one other Member refused to sign the volume. "We are not having our names handed down to posterity," she said, "tacked on to Sir Winston Churchill's. We remember Tonypandy." (In 1910, when Churchill was Home Secretary, troops were sent to Tonypandy in Wales to break up a coal strike there.)

After the local Labour Party in the 'Exchange Division' came under control of Bevanites it voted on March 27 1955 not to let Mrs. Braddock run in the May General Election of that year, because she had been too critical of Aneurin Bevan. However, its 'National Executive Committee of the Labour Party' ruled that she should be permitted to stand for election under the Party banner. In spite of a split in the Labour vote due to a Bevanite who ran as an independent, Mrs. Braddock was re-elected by a larger majority than previously.

Upon receiving an anonymous phone call regarding arms shipments at the Liverpool docks in December 1955, Mrs Braddock went to the docks and found an Egyptian freighter loading 1,000 tons of arms and ammunitions, tank tracks, and radio parts. It was then disclosed that obsolescent British arms had been shipped by foreign sources to Egypt and Israel. Following her discovery, the Foreign Office announced on December 31 1955 a halt on surplus arms shipments.

On one occasion Tory Quintin Hogg (later Lord Hailsham) called her his pin-up girl. The Exchange Labour group sent a letter of protest and a picture of Bessie. Hogg replied that he would have the picture framed. Such was the lighter side of the politics of the day. But it was the serious dimensions, which predominated. When criticised for having the Communist hammer and sickle flag on her car, Bessie described herself as "an international socialist" and continued by saying, "the flag means a lot to me."

In 1956 Bessie had been informed about the general welfare of the conditions of prisoners at Walton Gaol in Liverpool. She had the complaints investigated for several weeks and the resulting documents alleging ill treatment of inmates were sent to the Secretary of State for the Home Office. Bessie urged an immediate inquiry in which prisoners could make public statements. She was certainly no wallflower when she sat in the Chamber of the House of Commons, and at times, putting her point of view could be a little unorthodox. In order to protest about the widespread buying by juveniles of air pistols without licences, she fired two of them in the House in July 1956 after obtaining a licence for them, and explained: "You see I have to startle this House before anyone does anything about anything. I confiscated these pistols from the police in Liverpool Juvenile Court. I will hand them (the guns) back to the police and 1 will give back the licence because my tongue is good enough without a gun". When Bessie was a member of the House of Commons, newspapers and magazines were never short of something to write about. 'Time Magazine' May, 9, 1955 stated:

Mrs. E. M. Braddock weighs about 200 pounds and is a big, resolute-looking woman. She is the beloved and admired champion of her Liverpudlian constituents and she is as salty as Liverpool's docks, as fierce as its wind, and biting as its rain. She is a vigorous speaker, has a broad Lancashire accent. Mrs. Braddock's favourite hobbies are reading and housekeeping and in her spare time she models outsize clothing. She was an honorary officer of the British Professional Boxers Association and a past president in 1944 and also vice-president of the Liverpool Trades Council & Labour Party.

Her figure is stout, her bust formidable, and her manner blunt. Among the urbane Oxford and Cambridge tones of the House of Commons, her voice sounds rough and raucous as a Liverpool fishwife's. In the mannered cut-and-thrust of debate, her points are as emphatic as the slap of a wet cod across a face. Newspapers poke sly fun at her, other M.P.s snicker at her, county squires snort: "She's a disgrace to public life." But among her constituents in Liverpool's grimy dockland, Mrs. Bessie Braddock, M.P., is a beloved and admired champion.

For 210 lb. Bessie Braddock is a character in Liverpool—as salty as its docks, as fierce as its wind, as biting as its rain. Bessie was born 55 years ago in its working-class district, where one cold-water tap in the courtyard often served a whole block of houses. Her mother was a Labour Party worker and a social worker, ladling out soup from St. George's Plateau (atop the steps of a Liverpool concert hall), and one of Bessie's earliest memories is the look on hungry faces when the soup ran out. When she went to her first job at 15, she remembers her mother calling after her: "And don't come home until you join the union!" Bessie early dedicated herself to getting Liverpool's vermin-ridden, shivering, shawl-clad women and gaunt men out of their slums and into decent dwelling places.

The Liverpool Echo, November 17th 1987 stated:

The embodiment of Socialist Liverpool, Bessie Braddock J.P., M.P., loved and (sometimes) hated, became a legend in her own lifetime and one of the city's most fascinating characters. Bessie was taken to her first political meeting as a baby of three weeks, wrapped in her mother's shawl. Bessie also was with her mother on 'Bloody Sunday', in August 1911, when police charged thousands who had gathered to hear Tom Man speak at the transport workers' strike meeting. Bessie Braddock wrote: I joined the Communist Party because I was a rebel. I left the Communist Party for the same reason. I was a rebel and still am. The Communist Party hates social democracy even more than it hates Toryism.

She may have been nicknamed 'Battling Bessie', but she met royalty, Cabinet Ministers and top personalities and celebrities, and she never forgot her humble roots and was adored by the city's poor, the needy and unemployed. As Labour M.P. for Liverpool Exchange for 24 years, she fought like a tiger in political battles for the underdogs. Bessie could play the part of a lady when it suited her, but she could also use the language of the toughest. Among her army of friends were Harold Wilson, John Moore, Ken Dodd and Frankie Vaughan.

No M.P. has ever displayed such concern for the well being of her constituents as this plump and doughty fighter. Beneath the harsh exterior she often manifested, Bessie was one of the kindest of women. Her acts of compassion mostly unpublished are legion. In 1968 she became Vice-Chairman of the Labour Party. The following year she reached the summit of her amazing political career. In April 1970, Bessie was given the Freedom of her beloved city but was too ill to attend. Her sister, Mrs Enid Sharp, received the honour on her behalf. When Bessie died, on November 13, the same year, tributes galore were paid to her. One of the most touching came from a Liverpool flower-seller, whose family Bessie had helped long before, "Bessie was always good to the poor", she said, "if she saw a woman with a baby, who had no money, she would always give her a couple of pounds".

Bessie was a member of a Liverpool Joint Consultative Committee in 1960 when the items on the agenda were discussed in about fifteen minutes. The Committee Clerks were worried at having called distinguished Liverpool representatives to such a short meeting, but Bessie kept it going for another hour under any other business. A number of people expressed their affection for Bessie, one of her admirer's recalled his childhood, and the time he came into contact with Mrs Braddock:

My earliest recollection of Bessie Braddock takes me back to 1943, when I attended a hearing of the Public Assistance Board with my mother in Liverpool. My recently widowed mother with two children aged six and seven had to appear before the National Assistance Board to appeal against the refusal of her application for an increase in allowance, after the death of my Father.

Three members sat on the bench, one of which was Mrs Elizabeth Braddock MP. They had to consider whether a disputed individual claim would be granted. I don't know what the outcome was, I guess it was negative, I do know that my mother always recalled how Bessie had put her arm around her shoulder and asked if she had had any food at all today, then Bessie took us for a cup of tea and biscuit at the small café across the road in Dale Street. But more importantly, my mother always recalled how Bessie spoke kindly and respectfully to her.

In those times things were a little different for those

seeking benefit than they are today. Our home visit from one of the hated officials of the Assistance Board resulted in a claim rejection because we literally 'had jam on the table' which was considered to be a sign of relative affluence, and therefore left my mother with two alternatives. Allow me and my sister to be put into care, or go out to work as a domestic cleaner and leave her two children aged six and seven to manage as best as they could at home. She was forced to choose the latter.

The National Assistance Act 1948 and National Health Service Act 1946 came into effect from July 5 1848 and brought an end to the Poor Law. Public Assistance Committees ceased to exist and their functions were transferred to various Government and Local Government departments. Another man expressed his feeling for Bessie when he met her after being demobbed from the Army:

I met Bessie Braddock in May 1960 when I was travelling back from Germany, having been discharged from the army. I got on the train at Euston station and entered a carriage, which in those days had separate compartments. The only other person in the compartment was a rather heavy built woman wearing a fitted coat and her trademark black hat. Even though I was suffering from the effects of consuming half a bottle of celebration brandy, I never the less recognized Mrs. Braddock.

During the next 5 hours she spoke to me about working class life in Liverpool, and the problems facing those very many people, who were living in poverty, and what might be done to help them. By the time I reached Lime Street Station, I was almost completely free of the British Army indoctrination, which I had become very slightly tinged with. I never fully appreciated at the time the full significance of that conversation with the great woman. Within six months I had become somewhat more radicalised, to say the least I was intrigued by her introduction to Labour Party politics and determined to find out all I could about the subject. And more particularly how it could help to bring about change in the lives of those who were marginalized by the grinding poverty, which was the norm for so many at that time.

The next time I met Mrs. Braddock was in 1968, on the steps of Saint George's Hall in Lime Street, Liverpool. With some fellow political campaigners, I was taking part in an all night vigil and demonstration to highlight the awful situation that homeless people were facing in Liverpool every night at that time. The idea behind it was to give a public show of solidarity with those sleeping rough, and various well-known figures amongst 'the Great and the Good' were invited to visit the demonstration and express their solidarity. I was not surprised when they did not show up. However there was one exception, and that was Mrs. Elizabeth Braddock, M.P. This was not long before Bessie began a decline in her health but as always she demonstrated her solidarity and concern for the least privileged in our society.

'Battling Bessie' leading a street demonstration

Chapter 7

*M*argaret *B*eavan

*M*argaret Beavan was born at a time when access to good health for the majority of people in Britain did not exist. Bad housing and the lack of good food together with casual employment all played their part in the misery of so many. It was pioneers like Margaret who led the way to better health for all the people of this land. Margaret was born on 1 August 1877 in Liverpool, the eldest of the three children. Her father, Jeffrey Beavan was an insurance agent. In 1890 the Beavan family joined their father in America for 2 years with the intention of settling down in that country. One of her classmates was the future spiritualist and preacher, Maude Royden. Margaret went on to study mathematics at Royal Holloway College, during which time her father returned to England and died of typhoid.

Their house was a quiet one and Margaret Beavan's life at this time was neither romantic nor particularly exciting. Few English homes of the late nineteenth century provided much in the way of excitement for children, and theirs was an average, disciplined, middle class home. Margaret's mother was a quiet and rather frail little woman and with the absence of her husband in America, she was left to give her children guidance and direction. As was natural, she tended to devote herself to them, and expected their devotion in return. The bond between them was a very close one and developed sensitive qualities in the children at an early age.

The Beavan children were taught early in life to be generous to others, and they found opportunities for self-expression in various small acts of service. Mrs. Beavan, herself a born giver, was one of those women who could never be happy unless she was showing kindness to other people and giving to the poor. She gave gifts to her friends on all occasions, and to her children a wealth of affection and attention which gave one of them, at least, a conception of motherhood that inspired her all through her life.

Christmas was a very much-loved occasion for the Beavans and there was probably no family in Liverpool who put more concentrated effort and thought into this festival. Margaret adored Christmas and was always full of plans of her own for gift making. It was instinctive in her to work out her own schemes and she took infinite pains over the smallest details. Though up to a point she would follow the suggestions of others, particularly when she felt affection for them, she much preferred to have her own way. This preference became an absolute necessity, as she grew older. As it was, her ideas, her gifts to her friends and her activities in general, showed signs of individuality.

It was from her father that Margaret Beavan inherited the strong and practical qualities, which had such a great effect on her future career. It was her determination to succeed, together with her keen brain, which allowed her to grasp the essentials of life, and gave passionate attention to detail. These same qualities in her father had enabled him to rise quickly in his profession and may have brought him outstanding success had he lived to complete his career. Even as a child Margaret's initiative and driving force were outstanding, as she was not only strong willed but extremely intelligent.

The climate, in America, proved unsuitable for the two

younger children and at the end of two years Mrs. Beavan was obliged to return to England with them all. During their stay abroad the children were under the control of their governess and they had little contact with the American way of life. By the time they returned to Liverpool, Margaret had grown to adolescence and she found new values in the environment of her native city. She was sent to a public day school, Belvedere School, and she entered into its activities with great enjoyment. Very soon it was as though she had never been away from the city, and she settled down happily to a life which was active and full of interest.

Many children display strength of will at an early age, yet lack the direction that was very evident in Margaret Beavan. She had within her the spring of originality that is a real motive power, a force which, rising creatively in the individual mind, seeks an immediate outlet in action. One of Margaret's friends describing her said: "She was no mere dreamer, sturdily built, and, with a determined mouth and chin, she looked what, in part, she was, a practical minded person with her feet firmly placed on the ground and her mind was occupied with the affairs of every day."

Some of her friends felt that if she had been a son instead of a daughter, she would no doubt have followed her father's profession and made a name for herself in the business world. She turned all her practical abilities to account by using the generosity bequeathed to her by her mother. This impulse drove her continuously forward in the service of others.

Liverpool in the eighteen-nineties was a flourishing seaport city. Steam was still the chief energising power and Liverpool, as the connecting link between two important means of communication, the steam ships and the railway, owed the greater part of her prosperity to its power. But locally communications were, like most other provincial cities, untouched by mechanical power. Petrol and electricity had not yet made their appearance, though they were shortly to do so. The horse cab, the hansom, and the horse-tram, which connected the city with its outlying parts, were the only methods of travel within Liverpool itself.

Altogether, life flowed fairly evenly for children of the middle-classes in the 1890s. They were able to follow an undisturbed routine of duties and pleasures without any threat of world forces to disturb their security. It was the last decade of the nineties in which the provincial towns of England were able to enjoy such peaceful isolation. As the century drew to a close and the dawn of the twentieth century was about to appear, a war broke up the calm. In 1899 the Boer War in South Africa took place, ending in 1902 and mechanisation had taken a firm grip of the industrial and domestic life of cities and drove away for good the comparative quiet, which reigned there.

Margaret loved her home, and her city and was very conscious of her relationship towards them. This was encouraged by her Presbyterian religion, as she was a keen churchgoer and attended the Sefton Park Presbyterian Church where the Reverend John Watson (more widely known as lan Maclaren) was at that time the minister in charge. Margaret Beavan had an admiration for this vigorous-minded man, which amounted to hero worship, and she was very much inspired by his influence. It was no doubt through her church that she learned to express herself in idealistic phrases, for she loved to use her high-sounding words and sentiments. She had in herself a passionate idealism, which expressed itself in more than words. Margaret could see what poverty was doing to the poor in the new mechanical age. This was the driving force that needed her best form of self-expression and she was able to give it full play, which made her stand out from her peers.

Although serious-minded she had other temperamental traits very strongly developed. She was cheerful and she loved fun and parties where she was often the centre of the attraction. She had a quick temper which would as suddenly die out when its force was spent, but she could be exasperating at times when she was bent on some course of action. Margaret did not cherish resentment and neither did she expect others to do so.

She was almost entirely lacking in fear, and this, in itself, made her an outstanding person. It might have led her into all sorts of difficulties and scrapes if her serious-mindedness had not been so definitely a controlling influence. Margaret Beavan was not, at heart, a rebel. She had a reverence for institutions and never swerved in her loyalty towards them.

She did enquire rather earnestly into religious truth, for religion mattered a great deal to her personally, and until she could gain for herself a working theology she was not content. But for the most part she accepted the established order without wanting to change it as many independent-minded young people do. She was almost too evenly balanced in this respect and later in life it brought her some opposition for it seemed inconsistent to progressive-minded people that she herself should be so progressive in one way and at the same time so conservative in others. Miss Ashworth, a new teacher to Margaret's school, said she would never forget the day she arrived:

> On the afternoon before term began I arrived in Liverpool feeling rather strange and lonely for I knew no one at all there, and went to the rooms, which I was taking on from my predecessor. You can imagine the difference it made to me when I found these gay with flowers. My landlady told me that Miss Margaret Beavan had brought them. Margaret Beavan knew nothing about me except that I was a new mistress coming to a strange place, and she wanted me to have a welcome! That was very typical of her.

Perhaps there was something in this incident which made the first bond between them. At any rate from that time until she left school Margaret Beavan cherished a very great affection for this mistress who came to have a definite influence on the whole of her work. One of Margaret's closest companions who was at school with her, and remained her friend afterwards writes of this influence from her own knowledge:

> She (Margaret) was, I think, the most conscientious girl I have ever known, taking pains with whatever she had to do. She did attain some degree of mathematical skill before she went to college, but I now believe it was through sheer hard work and an intense desire to please Miss Ashworth, our beloved mathematics mistress.

This seemed further proved by the fact that Margaret took mathematics as her chief subject when she went to University and chose the college at which Miss Ashworth herself had studied, rather than to join her friend who was going to Somerville. In the realms of scholarship, the influence of her Belvedere School was, by her own admission, one of the most important in her life (The Liverpool High School), as it was then called.

Margaret's child welfare work was an important aspect of her life. She dedicated herself to the cause of sick children of the Liverpool poor. This was at a time when professional social work was in its infancy and training and research was an important element to further progress. Margaret herself was not trained, but her skills at organisation and her dedication to the society for which she worked made up for this. In working for the Liverpool Kyrle Society she was following in the footsteps of many middle class single women who, from the late 1860s onward, took up various forms of social work to raise physical and moral standards of the working classes, concern over which had grown as the nineteenth century progressed; increased urbanisation turned the working classes as a large mass of people seemingly divorced from the influence of the educated and civilised middle classes.

The advent of new unionism (the unionisation of those who were perceived as being unskilled) in the 1880s, and industrial unrest such as that of the dock strikes in London and Liverpool, only increased anxiety over this large section of society. Middle class women, regarding their domestic expertise as particularly suitable for social work, made themselves familiar with the lives and needs of the poor. This was at a time when Margaret was growing up, at the turn of the century and she took on work which had become acceptable for women to do.

She was not an academic high flier and had to make up for this by hard work. She was conscientious and popular, becoming Head Girl and was strongly influenced by her headmistress, Miss Huckwell, who encouraged her pupils to give back what they had been lucky enough to receive, something which Margaret later did when she addressed groups of young people as Lord Mayor. She encouraged girls to marry and have children as she felt it was their highest duty as women: "You are young and will probably marry in the future. It is the best thing to do. Don't remain an old spinster like me".

Margaret may have wanted to dedicate her life to a career in social work, but she was not the type of person to go against expert opinions, so she possibly sought advice in how best to help those less fortunate than herself and chose the political route. Another reason, then, could have been to do with her health, as from her teenage years she was plagued with a bad chest and had regular bouts of bronchitis. It is quite possible that she ruled out marriage herself, rather than it being ruled out for her by lack of suitors. I feel that this situation influenced her move to care for children, sickness brought out all her motherly qualities of care, compassion and the need to nurture. In her work for the Liverpool Child Welfare Association (the name changed from the Invalid Children's Association in 1924) she became the mother of many children by proxy. In one of her speeches as Lord Mayor, on her civic visit to Italy in 1928, she told a group of children: "I am not married. I am what they call in England a spinster and loving children dearly, I have looked after a large family for over twenty years".

She combined civic duty with civic motherhood, and it is clear that she was particularly proud of the title given to her of the 'Little Mother of Liverpool' by Archibald Salvidge. Margaret's involvement with disabled children began with a meeting at her old school. She had not at this stage a desire to work in this field, but needed to find a firm direction. She had done a little teaching at a local boys' school and took a Sunday school class at her church, but this did not seem to fully satisfy her. At a meeting in 1900 when Margaret was twenty-three she found out about the work of the Invalid Children's Association (ICA), a branch of the Liverpool Kyrle Society. Many notable people were members of the Society such as William Morris, pioneer of ecology. He became involved in the society, founded in 1875 to improve working-class housing and the wider environment, and the Common's Preservation Society, founded ten years earlier.

The Society had moved into the basement to teach a class of disabled children, whose education was normally neglected, at the Liverpool Women's Settlement in Everton, Liverpool. The first settlement houses were founded in the 1880s and were designed to bring betterment to the working classes, through contact with educated middle class volunteers. These appealed greatly to women interested in philanthropic work, bringing their special skills as domestic managers to the world at large and giving them freedom outside the confines of the middle-class home. Two ladies with previous experience at working with the poor set up the Victoria Settlement: Dr Lilias Hamilton, who first trained as a nurse at the Liverpool Workhouse, Brownlow Hill, and Edith Sing, who had worked at the Mayfield House Settlement in London

Margaret's opinions with regard to the poor remained firmly in the Victorian age as the twentieth century progressed. Other fields of social work were becoming more professionally based. Two years after Margaret began work at the Liverpool Settlement, Elizabeth Macadam took over as Warden. She was a trained social worker and she and Eleanor Rathbone set about reorganising its running and began careful research in the lives and living conditions of the poor. Their evidence ultimately led to the publication of 'The Disinherited Family', an argument for Family Endowment.

Their work highlighted the difficulty for women and their children when relying solely on one man's wage to support them, in Liverpool in particular, with the widespread use of casual labour based on the docks. Casualisation meant that a regular wage could not be relied upon, resulting in debt and a reliance on the pawnbrokers and credit for survival.

The surveys of Rowntree and Booth revealed that a significant proportion of the poorest families were in primary poverty and so had no means to save and be thrifty. As the twentieth century progressed, Margaret's methods and opinions were increasingly at odds with more progressive elements in the field of social reform. However she did have the help of many of the wealthiest families in Liverpool who supported the 'Invalid Children's Assocation'. Among them were the Rathbones, the Holts and the Stanleys, as well as other leading citizens in industry and politics, for example, Sir Archibald Salvidge, Sir Max Muspratt, Sir Frederick Bowring and Sir Alfred Paton. Given this type of support, Margaret felt secure in the value and correctness of her work, which helped her in dedicating her life to it.

When Margaret started work for the ICA it was working on a very small scale having less than a hundred children on its books. Great respect must be given to the voluntary visitors who worked on their own initiative, until Margaret Beavan joined the organisation. There was no central organisation coordinating the work, and as the new century progressed, the growth in work was putting a strain on the parent organisation. By 1907 the 'Invalid Children's Association' needed to branch out on its own. This happened on New Year 1908 and Margaret became its Hon. Secretary and the President was Mrs Arthur B. Rathbone. The Annual Report for 1908 not only set out the aims and objectives of the new ICA but also reveals a very clear moral agenda behind helping these children. The organisations objectives were:

> Medical advice and the directing of children to appropriate places for medical treatment; also providing food and tonics if necessary.
> To provide surgical equipment, such as special carriages (on loan or purchased in instalments).
> To arrange admission to suitable institutions for treatment i.e. Hospital, convalescent home or boarding out in cottages.
> Help provide forms of recreation. In general, to seek to ameliorate the conditions and brighten the lives of sick and suffering children throughout the city.

Whilst the child would receive the greatest attention, he or she would not be treated in isolation from the family, as they would receive attention and help in their homes. Such relationships not only made for the greater happiness and care of the children themselves, but eventually reacted on the community at large.

Margaret's work for the ICA was influenced by current

anxieties and campaigns over infant mortality and public health. How important her intervention was in public health, can be seen by what happened at the start of the Boer War in 1899. The physical health of the population was such that the rejection rate of volunteers for the war was 330 of every 1,000 being rejected as unfit for service for reasons such as heart trouble, weak lungs, stunted growth and bad teeth. The government responded by setting up an Inter-Departmental Committee of Enquiry to investigate physical deterioration which reported its finding in 1904.

It found that while standards of health in general were rising, in the congested urban inner cities the standard of health was very low, and Liverpool was a prime example with its poverty, overcrowding and poor housing. It meant that the State needed to intervene for the sake of Britain's future; the Liberal government added legislation, such as the 1902 Midwives Act, to produce a wide, though not comprehensive, body of law affecting child welfare, free school meals for needy children (1906), medical inspection in schools (1907) notification of births leading to visits by health visitors; and the Children's Act (1908) providing a wide number of measures. State action boosted and complimented the work of voluntary charities such as the ICA. Margaret believed in co-operation between charity, local authority and government as the best means of tackling social problems.

A major concern for Margaret and her team of volunteers and the ICA, was tuberculosis. Although the rate was falling gradually it was still a major killer. Children were particularly susceptible to non-pulmonary forms of the disease, in particular regarding those in joints and it was felt tuberculosis in bones and joints was caused by drinking contaminated milk which paralysed the affected limb, leading to death.

Liverpool Corporation tried to combat the problem of contaminated milk by appointing a City Bacteriologist in 1900 to inspect and licence dairies and inspect cowsheds. Despite this, milk contaminated with tuberculosis was still a problem after the First World War. The Committee on Physical Deterioration drew particular attention to tuberculosis in the slums and focused on the incidence of the disease in children.

The National Association for the Prevention of Tuberculosis, founded in 1898, worked to highlight the problem and from 1911 onwards, government action was taken to tackle the disease.

The ICA embarked on their first major scheme led by a very enthusiastic Margaret Beavan, The Liverpool Open-Air Hospital for Children, Leasowe, on the Wirral, for the treatment of osseous tuberculosis. A memorandum stating the case for a grant was drawn up by Margaret and Dr Hope (Medical Officer for Health for Liverpool), which was successful. The treatment of children with tuberculosis was a difficult one, as it could take several years and was a drain on ICA resources; there was also a waiting list for treatment.

A hospital run by the ICA catering for over 200 children lessened the list and meant that beds would have to be found at other institutions in the area (paid for by the ICA with parental contributions). As a hospital school, Leasowe was entitled to an annual grant from the Government, the rest being raised by subscriptions and donations. Leasowe was built in stages (opening in 1914 and finally completed in 1918) as and when the money was available, which was a general pattern. The Babies Hospital (for wasting babies) had to be situated in one of the wards at Leasowe in 1915, and finally moved (not to new premises as there was no money for this) to a converted house in Woolton, called Highfield, which had also been used during the summer of 1923 for holidays for worn out mothers and their babies.

It can be said that Margaret Beavan did much that was good and selfless in her life, but some people felt certain aspects of her character were a little disquieting. For example her close association with Sir Archibald Salvidge, who founded the Conservative Working Men's Trade Union. Many felt his organisation was dividing working class people. Her approval of Mussolini, the Italian fascist leader, also increased antagonism towards her. The effectiveness of voluntary charity was under scrutiny in the early twentieth century and it was seen by many as a piecemeal solution to many of the problems suffered by poor people. However she was not affected by the debate, and she concerned herself with helping children directly, while others attempted change to prevent this type of need from emerging in the first place. Margaret had a good heart and was convinced her methods would help those less fortunate than herself. She was convinced that the methods of the Child Welfare Association would eventually reduce poverty and want, but seemed to ignore the fact that they did not have the resources to help all children, and that the Child Welfare Association employees were frequently overworked because of all that was demanded of them.

Whether she believed in her image of the 'Little Mother', it is difficult to ascertain, or whether she needed reassuring that her actions were correct in the face of social and political change during the 1920s. In 1929 it is possible that those she had helped showed their gratitude and voted for her, and that she would also gain the votes of 'respectable' working class people by winning a seat in Parliament. Those who did not vote for her were either 'not respectable' or had been duped by the promises of the Labour party. This was a pious expression, used a hundred years before by John Gladstone when he built two schools, one for the respectable poor and one for the 'non respectable poor'.

Families who sought her help did so because there was no other alternative. The sight of sick children moved her only as far as seeing that they received treatment, but not questioning why they were deprived in the first place.

She filled her days with committee work, and seemed to have little time to sit and consider why there was a need for organisations such as the CWA. Within her circle of peers and superiors she was protected and possibly exploited. Margaret was so involved with her work that she never took the opposition to her as serious, which she should have done. She overestimated her popularity and the support of the working class. Her defeat in Everton, denying her a seat in Parliament, was a shattering blow to a person who had felt secure in her position in society and her relationship to the working class.

The 1929 general election was the first election where all women over 21 years became eligible to vote. The Catholic authorities were anxious to 'suss' out where the Liverpool constituency candidates stood in support for Catholic schools, and Downey sent a questionnaire to each of the candidates asking them their views, but Margaret Beavan refused to answer. She was in a fix because her constituency was a mixture of militant Protestants and militant Catholics. If she had said yes to the Catholics, she would have lost the support of the Protestants. By saying nothing, she lost the support of the Catholics. Word went out that the Catholics should support the candidate who had responded to the Downey questionnaire, and this resulted in helping to defeat Margaret.

The period from June 1929 to her death in February 1931 was a sombre one for possibly she had been shocked into becoming aware that changes were occurring, and she had just failed to notice, or had not sufficiently been alerted to them. After such a busy and productive life her end seemed to be a sad one. She remained bewildered at her failure to gain a seat in Parliament, but carried on her work as best she could. Her health finally failed her after a very cold winter. She died in a room she had at Leasowe Hospital at the age of 54. The people lined the streets to watch the funeral procession of 'the little mother of Liverpool'.

Chapter 8

Jessie Reid Crosbie

Jessie on left back row

An old sage once said, "Angels walk among us unaware" and when we see them at their work we do not always appreciate who or what the are. This can be said of so many wonderful people who gave their lives for the betterment of their fellow man. Jessie Reid Crosbie was a good example. She was born in the Everton area of Liverpool in September 1876. Her parents were James and Mary Crosbie, who came from Scotland, and Jessie was the third of their five children. She dedicated her entire life to teaching and was a well-known pioneer in education reform throughout the country and an active member of many local welfare groups. Jessie wrote:

> I wonder if any of my colleagues remember the day on which they changed from one school to another. I very vividly recollect that Monday in August, 1905, when I left the happiness and the comradeship of my eight years' service in a large school in a middle-class neighbourhood,

and changed to a small Infants' School in one of the most needy districts of our great city. I was really scared of my new task, young and untried, yet eager for this fresh field of service, I entered the building to be greeted by five women colleagues, who gave me a welcome I can never forget.

A group of teachers more devoted, earnest, kindly and efficient I have yet to meet. For 25 years, along with others equally devoted, we worked together. I marvel now at their patience with me, as I broke out in so many fresh places through the years. They were always anxious to co-operate and to help in every way. They "tholed" me, as our Scotch friends would say, and without their help very little, if any, of what we were able to do would have been accomplished.

I thank my God upon every remembrance of them. The children in the school were very mixed, some came from very good homes, children of professional people, business folk and shopkeepers. Some from quite clean, but often poorly furnished homes, but not sordid. The greater number were from poor, crowded dwellings, in condemned property, destitute and often vermin infested. There were five or six families in one house, with one tap (cold water, of course) and one toilet only for the use of the whole crowd. It was the condition of these little ones that touched our hearts and nerved our wills to help.

Will you understand when I say that they were "too old too young" and so also were their poor, ignorant and weary mothers. These were the children we had to help and to teach, but how? The task seemed colossal. Where to begin? That was our problem. Many came to school on cold winter mornings without any breakfast. We were able, in those early days, to provide cocoa, bread and jam. Some came so tired and weary that the warmth of the school building lulled them to sleep. Many had no beds at all, only old mattresses or old coats on the floor, and they had been roaming the streets till midnight, the poor tired little mites. Bristling as it did with difficulties, which baffled us all, or seemed to do so. To have been brought up in a good home by loving and wise parents is a heritage far beyond rubies. This had been ours and we determined in some way to make up for the loss of such to our little people.

Jessie was more than a dedicated teacher as she was concerned at the plight of the poor in the late nineteenth and early twentieth century. She believed that the complete wellbeing of the child was crucial and that in order to learn at school it was necessary to be clean, well rested and have access to wholesome food. She decided that the living conditions of her pupils were a factor in how each child would learn. She felt that the hungry, tired, half-dressed urchins who attended her school each day would not learn unless their general welfare was looked after. Jessie arranged meetings with their parents developing parenting fellowships to involve them in the education of their children. In those days of vast unemployment, the Parish did much. (It was the forerunner of our welfare state.) But even the Parish could not cope with the awful problem of neglected children, casual labour and bad housing and all the problems that were heaped on people, in many cases through no fault of their own. Jessie goes on to tell us how she and the school coped with the problem of poverty:

I shall always remember when School opened one Monday morning and the children found that some good fairy evidently had brought plants, flowers, new pictures and many other interesting things into the schoolroom. How they tiptoed past one table, saying in hushed tones, "Look, someone has made a parler." Their idea, of respectability was just that, having a parlour. It was no wonder that later on, when I had a room of my own, they always called it "The Missus' Parler."

Our first task was to clean and tidy up the big group of the neglected. The little folk helped. A piece of bright ribbon was the reward for those who had kept their hair in place with string. A pair of laces if shoes were cleaned. Laces were nicer than tape or string anyhow. A bright hanky if a clean piece of rag had been used.

Such simple things, but they worked miracles, and gradually a change came.

Before we had our school baths installed, it was our custom to wash some of our dirtiest children once a week in a dolly-tub in our warm basement.

It was Louie's turn and joyfully she came downstairs with me. Off came her poor, dirty underclothing (to be burned later) and I said "Pop in the tub, dear, you're going to have such a nice wash and then you are going to have these lovely new clothes for your very own."

To my surprise Louie screamed out "Oh, no, teacher, don't put me in there, I'll be such a good girl if you just give me one more chance." All my coaxing seemed of no avail, her piteous crying continued. I could not understand it, and then she said, "Oh, teacher, I don't want to be drownded".

You see, Louie only knew that their tub was used for unwanted kittens and pups, never for clothes, and certainly never for Louie. Another day it was our "hanky" parade. We had said that anything would do for a hanky as long as it was clean, but hankies must be used. We were amused one day when Annie brought a piece of crepe for her hanky. This afternoon Harry had not arrived and looking out for him I saw his mother dragging him along as he screamed and kicked. "He won't come, miss, unless I gave him his dad's hanky. Dad only has one. I have given him a clean rag, it's all I've got." Harry held up the remains of a little baby's first shirt. (Memories of a Victorian layette) and said, "Look what she calls a "anky". I'm not having this damned thing for a "anky, ahy'ow". "No, Harry, you're not," I said, and cutting the little shirt in two and, removing the bits of lace and ragged edges, I folded the two pieces into squares. I gave them to him. He took them proudly, put them in his pocket and went quietly and content to his class. "All show hankies, please." It seemed Billy could not pull his hanky out of his trousers pocket. I went forward to help, when to my surprise and amusement, he cried "Leave it alone, will yer, it's me shirt."

Then we would have a shoe parade. And small prizes for those who had the cleanest pairs. I told them to ask Dad to clean them, as Mum had plenty to do,

One day a lady from London came to see us. Tommy looked down and seemed fascinated by her shoes, and then said, "Eh, miss, did your Dad polish those?" "No, dear," she answered, "Well he must, teacher said so". Her dad was Prime Minister at the time. These stories could be multiplied, and here's another one. Each Monday morning for many years, after school was opened, we asked a few questions. Will all children who have not been washed all over the weekend come and tell me why. Always the same answer, no hot water, no soap, no washbasin and mother had no time, we got the same answer about clean clothes.

The hair was a very real problem in those very early days, one morning a woman came in during question time bringing with her a very dirty and poorly clad boy to be admitted to school for the first time. I asked her to sit down until I had finished, she listened and presently jumped up saying, "ere you I thought this was a slum school, I didn't know it was a high-class one. Yer not having my kid. Yer a lot too particular for me, see. I'll take im somewhere else, where they'll be glad to ave im. You've lost im". I followed her out, and guided her into my little parlour. Inviting her to be seated, I said, "Were you not ashamed when you saw how tidy and clean most of our children were?" "No, miss, I was not. I've no basin, no soap, or 'ot-water, and I can't get the kid any clothes, so there, but I'll take 'im 'ome. Don't understand anything about it, miss, do yer?" But I understood only too well.

Taking from my cupboard a set of clothing for her little boy (including shoes) I handed them to her, together with a piece of soap, a flannel and a piece of old towelling, and then giving her twopence told her to take her little boy to the hairdressers' opposite to get his hair cut. I sent her on her way, bidding her to try and bring him back, clean and tidy in the afternoon. She looked at me for a minute, and then at the parcel, and said, "Y'are soft, supposing I sells the clothes and spends the money. Now wot about it". "Well," I said, "you see, they are not mine, they belong to what we call God's Shelf. I never provided any of the clothes. I don't think somehow you will sell them. Her lips quivered and she went out slowly. They did not return in the afternoon, nor in the morning, but as I stood at the gate looking out for stragglers the next afternoon, a little boy whom I did not recognise at all, pulled my pinafore and said, "Ullo, there, teacher, I come". "But who are you?" "That kid wot yer gave twopence to, yesterday." Jimmy grew to be one of our best and brightest scholars. Never was God's Shelf, nor the kindness of many friends from all over the city, so honoured. Seven years went by, and then, to our joy, we were promised a new school.

Out we went into a temporary building, and early in 1914 we returned to our beautiful new home, wide corridors; a central Hall, well-lighted spacious classrooms, and a beautiful room for our nursery children. More washing facilities and better toilet accommodation, and a large playground. How happy we were, and so very proud of our new home. Our kindly Authority had been very good to us. We were all so grateful, parents, children, and teachers alike. To have been brought up in a good home by loving and wise parents is a heritage far beyond rubies. This had been ours and we determined in some way to make up for the loss of such to our little people. To bring some beauty, joy and brightness into their lives and then to proceed as we could, to teach them the rudiments of learning, this was our task.

The changes Jessie made were groundbreaking by helping to lead the way in changing the education system. She founded mother and father fellowships, the forerunners of the 'Liverpool Parent Teacher Association', and she introduced the first school bathhouse system in the country. It was managed by volunteers from the mothers' group and resulted in up to 30 children each day going home happy after a warm bath with their dirty clothes replaced by clean garments. Jessie also took care of the nutritional needs of her pupils, as she started a free daily milk scheme, by coaxing local shopkeepers into donating the produce.

She found that many of her pupils roamed the streets till as late as midnight and decided to institute a curfew. Any child found out of their homes after 7pm was often on the receiving end of a severe telling off from Jessie herself, as she regularly policed the curfew with other volunteers. Jessie campaigned to make the curfew more widespread and used the local media to get her message across. However, as the small inner city houses were already cramped and overcrowded, mothers did not welcome the idea of having all of their children in the house under their feet every evening The next problem she tackled was local children roaming the streets at night.

Jessie contacted Fr. Dukes of St Francis Xavier's Church, who also expressed concern about the problem of juvenile delinquency, which existed throughout the area. Between them, they initiated a plan to deal with the situation. A play centre was set up at Salisbury Street School opening at 5 o'clock every evening, and every pupil was expected to attend. All the Catholic children were also ordered to attend Benediction every evening at St Francis Xavier's Church. After the service at 7.30 pm Father Dukes led the children out of the church and Jessie led her children out of the school and with the help of the teachers from both schools, each child was taken home. Any odd truants spotted on the way, were collected, and escorted home as well. A group of parents was organised into patrolling the streets until the pubs closed. Jessie and Father Dukes maintained this curfew for many years.

The play centre at the school and the 'School Meal Service', were the first in the country. The scheme was officially adopted, first locally, then nationwide in the thirties and continued successfully for many years. Jessie also introduced the first nursery school in the country and the first parent-teachers' organisation. She had baths installed at the school at a time when hardly any houses in the district had bathrooms and the children were persuaded to use them. Mothers were invited to bring their young children in for a bath and arrange for the little ones to be looked after, while the mothers had a bath themselves or did their washing in the basement sinks.

M.B.E. awarded 1938

Jessie was headmistress at the Salisbury Street School for more than twenty-five years and was fondly remembered by her pupils. She never married and was awarded the MBE in 1938 for her contributions to educational practices and in 1942 received an honorary M.A. degree from the University of Liverpool. After retiring, she travelled the country, lecturing on education and writing many articles. She was a revolutionary, ahead of her time, seeing many of her ideas and schemes adopted nationally. She was a member of the 'Girl Guides', and for forty years she was a leader in the 1st Liverpool Company. She devoted her life to those less fortunate than herself and on her eightieth birthday several of the groups of which she was a member held parties in her honour.

After all her pioneering Jessie was very unhappy when she learned of the new 'Education Act of 1944', and the 'National Health Insurance Act.' Jessie tells us why her mind was troubled with the implementations of the new Education, and Insurance Acts, when she wrote:

There are two 'Acts of Parliament' today which cause much controversy and great concern, and which will cost millions for their implementation through the years. I refer, of course to the Education Act of 1944 and to the 'The National Insurance Act.' Wide as these are in their conception, and generous in their provisions, they are hardly worth the paper upon which they are printed, nor the years of labour given to their preparation by earnest, devoted and brilliant men and women, and certainly not the enormous amount required to fully carry out their clauses, unless it is recognised more generally throughout the whole country, by Politicians and people alike, how large and important a part the Home must play if the ultimate and lasting benefits of these two Acts are to be fully realised.

Do not think for a moment that we underestimate the fine work of all members of the Teaching Profession, from the Primary Schools to the Universities. Nor the labours of doctors and nurses, nor again the excellent work done in Churches, Sunday Schools and Youth Clubs of all kinds, when we say that the teachers who matter most in a child's life, especially in its infancy, are the parents in the home, and they are, or should be, the first guardians of its health. Without full and intelligent co-operation between the parents and the school, between the parents and the doctors, very little can be accomplished. How can this co-operation be secured?

For all other trades and professions, years of hard study, patient preparation and training of the very best is given, but hardly any at all in the noblest profession of all, parenthood. Most parents enter their high calling with no preparation for it of any kind, and commence this difficult task, the building up of a home and the training of little ones - without the slightest knowledge of the job. Many who have come from good homes carry on the fine tradition of their parents, but far, far too many are unable to do so, because of their lack of home training whatsoever. What is the result? Thousands of young people who could have been worthwhile members of our great community have, in spite of the schools, the churches, and youth centres, failed to become so. These young people often become the danger in our land - the delinquents.

The truth is, that nothing can possibly take the place of the good home, many things can help, but cannot possibly be its substitute. May I remind you of the important and telling words of the Queen Mother: "It is on the happiness of home and family life that the true worth and strength of a nation depend." We need to remember that, as a rule, our children spend only 5 hours daily in the place called school, but 18 to 19 hours in the school called home. Also, in addition, all weekends and holidays. In the home, also, there is the influence of heredity and environment, especially in the early years. These all count enormously throughout the child's life. As well as these, the only teachers most children have for the first five impressionable years are just the ordinary parents of our land. Some live up to the highest conception of their great calling, but far, far too many are either utterly ignorant of, or perhaps thoroughly careless about it.

We have boys and girls to-day leaving school very illiterate and unprepared for life, not because of any lack in our educational system, but owing entirely to the absence of any kind of training in their homes, or of any co-operation between the home and the school, I have always maintained that every child, of whatever class, should have the same kind of training as that provided for the highest and wealthiest in the land. If this kind of training cannot be given in the home, owing to poverty, lack of room, of space, or equipment, ignorance, carelessness, or the real weariness of their parents, then it ought to be given, in our schools. Surely commonsense ought to convince us of this. Habits of all kinds formed in early childhood usually last. "Train up a child in the way he should go." This training is what our Nurseries, Nursery Classes and Infants' Schools so excellently provide, but in many cases it is negatived in the child's home, and much thought, time and money are wasted.

We commenced milk service in our school many years ago. If you had come along at 10.15am any morning you would have seen all the children along with their teachers, sitting at table and desk spread with brightly coloured cloths, flowers in the centre, pretty cups and plates, children provided on alternate mornings with hot milk or hot Horlicks and always two biscuits. Of course, the children enjoyed their lunch, but we really had not set out merely to let them drink milk, but to teach them how to drink it, to empty their mouths before drinking, to learn to use a cup with a handle, eat quietly and cleanly, and then, according to their age, to wash cups and plates and put all tidily away. It was a very important part of our daily curriculum. Most of the mothers paid 3d. weekly for each child. Not all could do so, of course. So then the charge was probably 2d. for Billy, 1d. for Mary, half a penny for the little one in the Nursery.

We encouraged them to pay if they could, but no child went without lunch. "How did you foot the weekly bill?," you are saying. Well once again our good friend came to our help. Every week he asked the amount of loss 5/- 7/6, 10/-, or perhaps more. Each week he paid the deficit, kindly, and unassumingly, saying as I thanked him, "You give the guts, miss, and I'll give the gold, but no one is to go without lunch ever whilst I am about." What a good neighbour. Teatime, and Tommy runs off home. Dad is eating his meal of potato pie and by his side is his jug of beer. Tommy watches, then, "Dad, you mustn't drink until your mouth is empty, teacher says so." "Now, me lad, none of that ere. Yer at "ome. None of yer 'igh-falutin' ways 'ere. Yer not at school now remember."

So Tommy, and many more like him grew up with two standards of behaviour the high one of the school, and very often the low one of the home. The little child was confused and because of the influences I mentioned earlier, the home won, and so it always will. It was just the same with speech training. Every effort was made in school to encourage the child to speak properly, but back in the home and in the street, the child quickly reverted to the language (including swearing) and the bad habits of his environment. We had to train our little folk in the clean and right use of the toilets, and we had wonderful results in school, then Tommy goes home, one toilet for the use, sometimes, of 30 adults and children. What about our careful teaching? With every good habit we tried to inculcate the same result was experienced. Not with all but with many.

How to make the excellent training given in the school of lasting benefit? This was our problem. It was the same story with our Medical Services, in many cases, the doctors advised the mother to see that Mary is sent early to bed (Mary has nervous disability). Mother listens but she has no intention of taking his advice. Mary's late hours continued. Medicine is ordered and supplied, and because John kicks and screams and refuses to take it, the bottle and its contents are thrown out. The child is taken to the clinic, treatment is ordered, and for a day or two followed, but mother is tired or neglectful and the child's ailments return. What a mad, mad waste.

In our Hospitals and Convalescent Homes are hundreds of children who need never have been there. It is very often owing to the sad lack of parents' knowledge, or their carelessness about the duties and privileges of their high calling that these things occur. I could give many other instances, but these will suffice. What were we to do? Only one thing. Why had we not thought of it long ago? Bring the mothers into school and see if they and the teachers together cannot make something of it all. So began many years ago our Parent-Teacher Association.

We called it in the early days our Mothers' Fellowship. Such a humble, simple, effort, but what marvellous results. An addressed letter in an envelope was sent to every mother asking her to come along on the following Thursday afternoon and to bring the baby, or babies, with her. We were to have tea, some music and a simple talk together about the children and the home. I recall our first meeting very well. Our large central hall was clean and bright with plants and flowers, chairs had been provided by our Authority. Mothers ought to have every comfort possible, treat her with respect and your task is well begun. To that first meeting 40 mothers came. Many of our very best mothers, and some with no idea of their task, bringing one or more children with them (the toddlers had small chairs). We shook hands with each mother on arrival, saying how pleased we were to meet her. Then we were ready to start the great adventure. Some of them looked at us with suspicion. "What is it?" "Why has she asked us to tea?" I could sense their questionings, and I fully sympathised with them.

They had often been in our school at various functions. "You are all wondering why we have invited you to the school today," I said. "Well, I want you if you will, at these meetings to tell me what you are trying to teach your children at home, and then to listen whilst we tell you what we are trying to teach them in school. We want you to remember, mother, that your teaching is more important. We cannot carry on successfully unless we do meet like this, because whilst some of you are doing your part well, some are not quite pulling their weight. So our work here is of very little use. We are not blaming you, we only wish to help you, and you can help us too".

"Well, missus, what d'yer want us to do?" said one. And so we began a cup of tea, scone and butter, biscuits for the little ones. (These provided by a well-known city firm every month.) Then some music, singing or recitation. Only the best was given for only the best was good enough. Then followed a simple talk on some aspect of Infant Welfare and Child Training, Difficulties in the Home, How to Deal with Older Boys and Girls, etc. Not many questions were asked at the beginning, but soon confidence was gained and many joined in our simple discussions. We had many moving experiences. "What's the matter, mother, why are you crying?" "I can't help it, missus, I'm so happy, this place is like heaven." "How?" I said. "It is so warm and light, and that music, too. Don't let her stop playing miss, please." This mother's one window in a Court was stuffed with rags and her only light a smoky lamp or a bit of a candle. What was the music? Beethoven, Mendelssohn, Sibelius, etc. Of course, we had Community Singing, as well. I remembered some, old-fashioned lines:

> Touched by a loving hand,
> Wakened by kindness,
> Cords that were broken
> Will vibrate once more.

How many broken cords had re-vibrated during the years we shall never know, but we were glad, all of us, that we had been enabled to play our little part in these happy gatherings. Each meeting concluded with singing of the first and last verses of 'Abide with Me,' and a simple word of Blessing. The mothers were invited to come to the meeting half an hour earlier, and to go round and see their little ones in their classes, and to talk over any difficulties together with the teachers. They, and we, found these talks most helpful as time went by.

We met monthly and our meetings steadily grew in numbers owing entirely to the members' efforts. Before the 'Second World War' over three-hundred and fifty mothers belonged to our Fellowship, and attended regularly. So that all mothers, especially those who had to go out to work, could have a chance of advice and help, we held three of the meetings in the evening, when a similar programme was arranged; each mother paid a membership fee of 2d. and received a pretty card with our motto "That they all may be one." They hung these cards in their homes, and very proud they were of them. Each new baby received a Cradle Roll Certificate when mother brought him, or her, to the meeting for the first-time. Some of our older children sang a song of welcome to the little newcomer.

We had talks given by doctors, nurses, inspectors, from both the Ministry of Education and from our Local Authority, Talks on First Aid in the home, Care of the Sick (demonstrations given by some older club members), Food Values, Laundry Lessons, Invalid Cookery, or Ordinary Cookery, given by an expert, not using gas or electric but just the oven or the open fire, and many other subjects. Every kind of home need was discussed and every friend who could help came along so that mothers could receive every assistance in the part they had to play in the training of their big families. We often said to them, "Mother, do you remember the day God gave you your first little one? Well, that day He crowned you as queen, and daddy as king, and that dear little baby was your first subject. Your rule had commenced in your Kingdom called Home. It depends on how you and daddy rule together whether or not we are able to do our best for your little one when his school days commence with us."

In addition to our monthly gatherings the mothers were in and out of the school every day. The little side door was always open. Over the door leading into the Nursery Corridor we had a large poster 'Welcome All Who Enter'. "I suppose", said one very poor mother, "that notice there is for them big folk wot come along." "Yes, it is" I said, taking her by the arm, "come along in and welcome." All the children in the Nursery Classes had to be bathed by their mothers each week in our own School Baths. Mothers attended at times convenient. Plenty of hot water, good soap, sponges, face cloths and large towels were provided. The Bathroom was in charge of the members of our Fellowship Committee. These mothers gave a half, or a whole day, each week to serve in this way. Mothers were allowed to bring their very little ones and bath them under the supervision of the mother in charge.

The Committee women were later provided with white coats, with the letters M.F. embroidered on the pocket; they were very proud of these symbols of their office and kept their coats always clean. Different mothers did the washing of all towels each week, without any charge at all to the Authority. The baths and the bathroom were kept sweet and spotlessly clean by the mother in charge. I must tell you of a very touching incident of those days. One day an important clerical gentleman came to visit us. Taking him along to the bathroom I remarked, "I wonder if you will give a word of special praise and encouragement to my friend in charge-to-day.

She comes once every week and baths all the motherless children, or those whose mothers are sick or at work. She looks over the parcel of clean clothes sent along from the little one's home. She puts on tapes and buttons as they are required. Darns socks and won't have a word of thanks. If some little one is very poorly clothed she usually has found some garments to replace the badly worn ones. You know her kindness will very splendidly illustrate your text for a coming Sunday. 'Inasmuch as you have done it unto one of the least of these'." Then he approached my helper and tried to thank her loving and unselfish service. I can never forget her answer and I quote it in all humility: "Don't listen to her, Sir, don't take no notice of her. She has given us just ordinary women a chance to do a little bit of what them big ladies is always doing." After a few months' work with our fellowship we began to notice a great change in the appearance and the behaviour of many of our poorest and neglected children. There was now no excuse for them to be dirty.

The baths were available for all who needed them. If no hot water at home, plenty in school. These mothers had never had a chance before to be really clean, now they grasped their opportunity with both hands. Do not mistake me, the change did not come suddenly, slowly but surely the home standards were rising and our hearts were made glad. Children's clothes were clean and tidy. The hair of many children shone like gold. What a change! A new day had dawned in that dark and dreary district. I think a story can illustrate this well and show what a remarkable change had come over many of our mothers. We had a lady M.P. with us one morning and she was very interested in all she saw and heard. As she expressed a wish to say a word to the mothers, we very quickly gathered a group of about 100 women to meet her. The visitor's question was to the point. "What difference has the Mothers' Fellowship made in your lives?" There were many answers, I just quote three. "The Fellowship has made ladies of us." "The Fellowship has made us matter." "The Fellowship has made us into mothers of very importance." This last answer told us that in some little way we were succeeding in our task in helping the mothers to rule their kingdom called Home. But only half of our work was being done. Mothers were striving to do their best.

Yes, but what about father?

This is another story.

In 1961 Jessie was knocked down while crossing the road and was taken to Stanley Hospital in Liverpool and later to Southport Nursing Home where she died the following year aged eighty-two. The school and houses in the area were demolished in slum clearance in the nineteen-sixties and blocks of high-rise flats were built on the site. The only Memorial to this remarkable woman was the naming of one of the blocks 'Crosbie Heights' and this was at the insistence of local residents. The flats have now made way for a modern estate of houses of which Jessie would have approved.

Chapter 9

𝒪leanor 𝒪Rathbone

𝒪leanor was the second daughter of social reformer William Rathbone the VI and his second wife, Emily Lyle. Eleanor Florence Rathbone was born in Liverpool on 12 May 1872. She was a Member of Parliament and long-term campaigner for women's rights. Eleanor was strongly influenced by the dedication of her father to help those less fortunate than herself. She was an acknowledged social reformer and advocate of women's suffrage. She went to Kensington High School, London, and later studied in Somerville College, Oxford.

After graduation, she worked alongside her father investigating social and industrial conditions in Liverpool until William Rathbone died in 1902. Eleanor continued the work and published their report on the results of a special enquiry into conditions of labour at the Liverpool Docks. She first made her mark in 1903 when she reported this to the Poor Commission and finished her report with the statement:

Finally, I wish to say, although with a strong sense of temerity of expressing an opinion on so limited experience, that the evils of the present system of casual labour seem to me so great and the chance of remedies being adopted on a sufficiently effective scale, seem so small that in spite of a strong bias in favour of individual effort I have been driven to the conclusion that the final remedy lies in the taking over of the whole work of loading or unloading ships in the port by the corporation or the Merseyside Docks and Harbour Board, or by other public body with a representative element.

She was Liverpool's first woman Councillor, winning Granby Ward as an independent in 1909, a position she held until 1934. Her life's work was dedicated to solving social problems that beset poorer families and her work as a Granby Ward Councillor helped codify her ideas for social reform. During World War I, she organised the Soldiers' and Sailors' Families Association and was responsible for distributing allowances to those who had men in the forces. This experience gave her a practical understanding of how to implement a system of family allowances. In 1917 she founded the Family Endowment Committee, which concerned itself with the condition of poor families.

In 1924 she published a book 'The Disinherited Family' which argued that the State should subsidise poor families via a system of family allowances. When she became Representative in 1929 for the Combined Universities she established the perfect platform to pursue her campaigns against poverty. Family allowances came to fruition under the Attlee Government of 1945 when the Family Allowance Act was passed. During her career she was member of various Committees including Chairman of Family Endowment Society, Member of the Children's Minimum Council and Joint Committee on Refugees. She was also a particularly vociferous campaigner for issues that directly affected women.

In 1934 she published her first book 'How the Casual Labourer Lives' and also wrote a series of articles for a suffragette magazine, 'The Common Cause'. In 1913 she founded the Liverpool Women Citizen's Association to promote women's involvement in political affairs. At the outbreak of World War I, Eleanor organized 'The Town Hall Soldiers' and Sailors' Families' Organisation', to support wives and dependents of soldiers. She formed the 1908 Club, (still in the Adelphi Hotel, Liverpool), reputedly the oldest women's forum still in existence.

She also opposed violent repression in Ireland and was instrumental in negotiating the terms of women's inclusion in the 1918 Representation of the Peoples Act. In 1919, when Millicent Fawcett retired, Eleanor took over the presidency of the National Union of Societies for Equal Citizenship (renamed NUWSS), and as such was responsible for the creation of the Liverpool Personal Service Society (PSS).

She also campaigned for women's rights in India and in 1924 in the 'Disinherited Family', she argued that economic dependence of women was based on the practice of supporting variably-sized families with wages that were paid to men, regardless of whether the men had families or not. Later she exposed insurance regulations that reduced married women's access to unemployment benefits and health insurance. In 1929 she entered Parliament as an Independent Member for the Combined English Universities, when one of her first speeches was about clitoridectomy in Kenya. During the depression she campaigned for cheap milk and better benefits for the children of the unemployed. In 1931 she helped to organize the defeat of a proposal to abolish University seats in Parliament and won re-election in 1935.

Eleanor Rathbone had realized the nature of Nazi Germany and in the 1930s joined the British Non-Sectarian Anti-Nazi Council to support human rights. In 1936 she warned about a Nazi threat to Czechoslovakia and she became an outspoken critic of appeasement in Parliament. She denounced British complacency in Hitler's remilitarisation of the Rhineland, the Italian conquest of Abyssinia and the Spanish Civil War. Once she tried to hire a ship to run the blockade of Spain and remove republicans at risk from reprisals. Her determination was such that junior ministers and civil servants of the Foreign Office would reputedly duck behind pillars when they saw her coming. She supported the views of Winston Churchill and Clement Attlee, but earned the hostility of Neville Chamberlain.

On September 30 1938, Eleanor denounced the recently publicized Munich Accord (an agreement to appease Hitler). She pressured Parliament to aid the Czechs and grant entry for dissident Germans, Austrians and Jews. In 1939 she set up a Parliamentary Committee for Refugees to deal with individual cases from Spain, Czechoslovakia and Germany. During World War II she regularly chastised Osbert Peake, Undersecretary at the Home Office, and in 1942 pressured the government to publicize evidence about the Holocaust. The year before her death in 1945, she was delighted to see the Family Allowance Act become law. Eleanor died January 2 1946.

Eleanor is still remembered by the many institutions and buildings named after her, examples being, the Eleanor Rathbone Building, and the Eleanor Rathbone Theatre in the University of Liverpool.

Chapter 10

*C*harlotte (Lottie) *D*od

*W*e may not find any reference to Charlotte Dod, or 'Lottie' as she became known, making her mark in Liverpool. Her father made his living in the cotton trade and in banking in the town so the family was very rich and Lottie had a privileged life, with access to sporting facilities that would be denied most children in the nineteenth and early twentieth century. She also had remarkable sporting talent, which could not be acquired through wealth alone. Lottie was determined to succeed in her chosen sports of tennis, archery, golf, skating, tobogganing and hockey. In many ways she was a pioneer of women's rights in the field of sporting events. She was strong, and not afraid of hard work and failure was not part of her make-up. She had the determination of Grace Darling, who used just a rowing boat in heavy seas, to rescue nine sailors in 1838.

She was tall and athletic, and she started her tennis career at the age of 11. She made her debut in tennis together with her sister Annie who was eight years older, when they entered their first tournament, in the Northern Championships in Manchester. They lost in the first round of the doubles tournament, but won in the consolation game. One journalist wrote that Miss Lottie Dod should be heard of in the future. Slowly Lottie became an established top player, illustrated by the fact that she partnered the then seven-times Wimbledon doubles winner Earnest Renshaw for the first time in 1887. She became the youngest of major tennis champions at 15 by winning Wimbledon. Beating the defending champion, Blanche Bingley, she also won the Irish tennis title in 1887. Lottie played hockey and golf representing Britain in International Hockey in 1889 and 1890 and winning the British Ladies Championship in 1904 at Troon in Scotland, where she defeated May Hazlet in the final.

She was also exceptional at archery where she was an Olympic silver medallist in 1908. She remains the youngest player to win the women's singles tournament and the press dubbed her as "Little Wonder". She is also named in the 'Guinness Book of Records' as the most versatile female athlete of all time. Lottie remains the youngest ladies' singles champion, though Martina Hingis was three days younger when she won the women's doubles title in 1996.

She was one of the most remarkable sportswomen of her, or any other, generation. Winning the Wimbledon tennis singles on five occasions, she was awarded the British ladies' golf crown, then represented England at hockey, and was of the highest standard at toboggan and skating.

Charlotte Dod was born on 21 September 1871 in Bebington, Wirral, the last of four children. By the turn of the century Lottie was pleading for suitable attire for women's tennis, which would not impede breathing. She was well qualified to take the lead in her campaign for shorter and more comfortable dresswear, on behalf of all sportswomen, given her ability in a range of activities. Lottie wrote of her feelings about the type of dress women had to wear while taking part in the sport of tennis in 1897:

> The ladies' dress is always more or less of a trial while
> taking exercise, and the blessings of our sex would be

heaped upon any one who could invent a more comfortable garment. As the skirt must be endured, it is important to have it made somewhat short, reaching to the ankles, and equal in length. That is, seemingly equal, but in reality a lawn tennis skirt should be cut half an inch or an inch shorter at the back than at the front. It will then appear uniform in length all round, and will not trip you up when you run backwards in volleying say, a high lob, which skirts, as ordinary made, are much inclined to do. It should be about three yards wide. If less, it would be rather apt to catch, when one makes sudden springs from side to side, as in volleying and if wider, the wind blows it about and perhaps hits the racket when we fondly imagine we are going to drive the ball.

Lottie won the British Ladies Amateur Golf Championship, played twice for the England women's national field hockey team (which she helped to found) and won a silver medal at the 1908 Summer Olympics in archery.

The family was wealthy enough to provide for all their children for life so that Lottie and the rest of the siblings, Willy, Annie and another brother, Tony, never had to work during their lifetime. Just like their sister, they all excelled in sports. Annie was a good tennis player, golfer, ice skater and billiards player. Willy Dod won the Olympic gold medal in archery at the 1908 Games, while Tony was a regional archer and a chess and tennis player. When Lottie was nine years old, two tennis courts were built near the family's estate, Edgeworth.

Lawn tennis was invented in 1873, and was highly fashionable for the wealthy in England, so all of the Dod children started playing tennis. In the 1885 tournament, Lottie came to prominence when she nearly beat reigning Wimbledon champion Maud Watson in the final, losing 8 – 6, 7 – 5. Only six competitors, not including top player Watson, entered. Lottie easily advanced through the first rounds to earn the right to challenge the defending champion Blanche Bingley, whom she defeated 6–2, 6–0. The two would meet again in the final of the 1888 West of England Tournament. Although designated as a so-called "open" tournament, the officials made the remarkable decision to impose a handicap of 152 on Lottie. She still managed to win against her opponent, Blanche Bingley. The Wimbledon final of 1888 was a rematch of the previous year, and Lottie again emerged victorious (6–3, 6–3). Lottie's style of play was regarded as unorthodox, but now seems notably modern. She was perhaps the first player to advocate hitting the ball just before the top of the bounce and to adopt a modern, single-handed racquet grip. Her groundstrokes were reported by contemporaries to be unusually firmly hit by the standards of the time.

Like many female players of the day she served underhand and only rarely employed spin. Lottie only entered one open tournament in 1889, the Northern Championships, which she won. She decided not to play at Wimbledon in 1889 much to the disappointment of her fans. Together with her sister Annie and some friends, she was on a sailing trip off the Scottish coast, and did not want to return in time for Wimbledon. This was followed by a complete absence from the game in 1890. Lottie was determined to win the 'Wimbledon Championship' in 1891. Although it was her only competitive appearance of that season, she won her third Wimbledon title with ease, by defeating Hillyard (6–2, 6–1). In 1892 Lottie suffered her first singles defeat in an open tournament since 1886, losing to Louise Martin of Ireland in the Irish Championships.

This was the last of only five losses in her entire tennis career. Lottie continued to play strongly throughout the year, culminating in another easy Wimbledon victory over Hillyard. Her last tennis season as a competitive player was 1893, and she played in just two tournaments, winning both. On each occasion, she defeated Blanche Hillyard in three sets, despite a heavy fall in the Wimbledon final. Her record of five Wimbledon titles would not last for long, as Hillyard, after losing in the final to Lottie five times, won her sixth title in 1900. Suzanne Lenglen broke Lottie's record of three consecutive singles wins by winning from 1919 to 1923. Apart from entering women's tournaments, Lottie sometimes also played and won matches against men who usually played with a handicap, and on one occasion defeated star players Ernest Renshaw and George Hillyard (the husband of Blanche) when doubling with Herbert Baddeley. Lottie's Wimbeldon record was:

Grand Slam Singles Finals Wins (5) Year
Championship Opponent in Final
Score in Final

1887	Wimbledon	Championships	(1)	Blanche Bingley	6-2, 6-0	
1888	Wimbledon	Championships	(2)	Blanche Bingley	6-3, 6-3	
1891	Wimbledon	Championships	(3)	Blanche Bingley	6-2, 6-1	
1892	Wimbledon	Championships	(4)	Blanche Bingley	6-1, 6-1	
1893	Wimbledon	Championships	(5)	Blanche Bingley	6-8, 6-1, 6-4	

Although tennis would remain Lottie's favourite sport, she shifted her attention to other activities in 1895, when she joined her brother Tony on a trip to the winter sports resort of St. Moritz, which was very popular with English travellers. Lottie passed the St. Moritz Ladies's Skating Test (figure skating), the most prestigious skating for women at the time. She also rode the toboggan on the famous St Moritz Cresta Run, and began mountaineering with her brother, climbing two mountains over 4,000 m in February 1896. After a long cycling trip in Italy, Lottie and Tony returned to England, only to return to St Moritz in November, now accompanied by their mother and brother, Willy. This time, Lottie took the St. Moritz Men's Skating Test and passed, as the second woman ever. She also competed in curling.

In the summer of 1897, she and Tony again ascended several mountains, this time in Norway. The sport of women's hockey was still new when Lottie took up the game in 1897. She was one of the founding members of a women's hockey club in Spital. Playing as a centre forward, she was soon named captain of the team. Club matches in which she played were won, while losses happened only in her absence. By 1899, Lottie achieved captaincy of the Cheshire county team, and represented her club at meetings of the women's hockey association for the northern counties. She first played in the English national team on 21 March that year, winning 3–1 over Ireland. Both English goals in the 1900 England and Ireland rematch were scored by Lottie, securing a 2–1 victory.

She failed to attend the match against Wales, suffering from sciatica attacks which kept her from sport for months. Although she had recovered by 1901, Lottie would not play again in national or county matches. All members of the Dod family stopped attending sports events for a while after their mother died on 1 August 1901, and Lottie apparently lost her interest in field hockey during that period, although she did occasionally play for the Spital Club until 1905.

Golf Clubs allowed women to play about the time Lottie first played golf at age of fifteen. Unlike tennis, Lottie found it a difficult sport to master. By the time she became seriously interested in the sport, the Ladies Golf Union (LGU) had been founded, and women's golf had become a real sport. Lottie helped establish a ladies' golf club at Moreton, Wirral in 1894 and entered that year's National Championships (match play) at Littlestone (Kent). She was eliminated in the third round, but her interest in the sport grew, and she became a regular competitor in the National Championships and other tournaments for the next few years. In 1898 and 1900 she reached the semi-finals of the National Championships, but was defeated narrowly both times. In 1900, she also played in an unofficial country match against Ireland, which the English team won 37–18.

Lottie did not compete in golf in 1901, and hardly entered major tournaments in the next two years, but she did play in the 1904 National Championships, held at Troon, Scotland. She qualified for the semi-finals for the third time in her life, and won the finals for the first time. Her opponent in the final was May Hezlet, the champion of 1899 and 1902. The match was very close, and the two were tied after 17 holes. Hezlet narrowly missed her putt on the final hole, after which Lottie gained an unexpected victory, becoming the first, and to date only, woman to win British tennis and golf championships. Following her victory, Lottie sailed to Philadelphia, where Frances Griscom a former American golf champion, had invited her to attend the American Ladies Championship as a spectator.

Upon arrival, Lottie found the tournament regulations had been changed to allow for non-Americans to compete, and she was requested to do so. Her loss in the first round was a disappointment, but she persuaded several Americans to come and play in the British championships the following year, 1905. In the week before, these three international matches were planned, starting off with the first British-American one. Lottie was the only British player to lose a match, as the United Kingdom won 6–1. She then played for the English team in a 3–4 defeat against Scotland and a 4–3 win over Ireland, although she lost both her matches. Lottie was then eliminated in the fourth round of the National Championships. It was to be her last appearance in golf.

In 1905, Lottie and her brothers sold 'Edgeworth' in the Wirral and moved to a new home near Newbury, Berkshire. They had been practising archery but all three took it more seriously by joining the Welford Park Archers in their home town, Newbury. As one of their ancestors was said to have commanded the English longbow men at the Battle of Agincourt, they found this an appropriate sport. Lottie won her first tournament in 1906, and finished fifth in the Grand National Archery Meeting of 1906, 1907 and 1908. Lottie's performances in the 1908 season earned her a place in the British Olympic team. The field in the women's archery event consisted only of British women, but without the best archer of the era, Alice Leigh. Lottie led the competition, held in rainy conditions, after the first day but was surpassed by Queenie Newall on the second day, eventually taking second place with 642 points to Newall's 688.

Her brother Willy fared better and surprisingly secured the gold medal in the men's competition. In 1910, Lottie came close to winning the 'Archery Grand National', which would have made archery the third sport in which she became a national champion. Both Lottie and her brother William led after day one, but moved down to second on the final competition day. After the Welford Archers were disbanded in late 1911, the Dod's interest in archery faded, meaning the end of Lottie's long competitive sports career. Later in 1913, Willy and Lottie moved to a new house in Bideford (Tony had married in the meantime).

When World War I broke out, Willy enlisted with the Royal Fusiliers, while Lottie worked for the Red Cross in a military hospital in Speen, Berkshire. Lottie wanted to be transferred to the war zones in France but was hampered by sciatica and never served as a nurse outside of England. She did receive a Service Medal by the Red Cross for serving more than 1,000 hours during the war.

Lottie, and other past Wimbledon Champions, were presented with a sterling silver commemorative medal on the Centre Court at the 'All England Lawn Tennis and Croquet Club', by King George V and Queen Mary, at the Silver Jubilee Championships of 1926. Lottie met many of her old opponents some of whom she had not seen for twenty years and more, including Maude Watson and Blanche Bingley.

Lottie was noted for a fine singing voice and for some years in the twenties and thirties was a member of two distinguished choirs, 'The Oriana Madrigal Society' and 'The Bach Cantata Club', performing in many concert halls around London. She sang with the Bach Club when it gave a recital before King George V and Queen Mary, in the Chapel at Buckingham Palace on Wednesday 16th March 1927. No record of the programme or the performance now exists. At some time or other Vaughan Williams heard Lottie sing solo, because a note among her papers mentions that the composer had liked her voice.

In later years Lottie made her home in London and Devon, and never failed to attend the Wimbledon Championships until she was in her late eighties. After her brother Willy died in 1954, she lived in several nursing homes on the English south coast, eventually settling at the Birchy Hill Nursing Home in Sway. There she died, unmarried, aged 88, passing away while listening to the Wimbledon radio broadcasts in bed, on June 27th 1960.

Chapter 11

$\mathcal{D}$ame $\mathcal{M}$ay $\mathcal{W}$hitty

$\mathcal{M}$any children over the years will have seen May Whitty, she was the kindly farmer's wife on television in the film 'Lassie Come Home' first released in 1951. In her first talking film, 'Night Must Fall', shown in 1937, May played the part of a foolhardy lady who falls for the charms of homicidal Robert Montgomery.

Dame May Whitty, was born Mary Louise Whitty on June 19th 1865 in Liverpool. Her father was Alfred Whitty the youngest son of Michael James Whitty, the founder of 'The Liverpool Daily Post' and founder of the Liverpool Police Force and Fire Service in 1836. Alfred married Mary Aston, a Lancashire woman, and they had three children, May being the youngest. The young May Whitty was adventurous and determined and had the same discipline for detail as her grandfather, Michael James Whitty.

May's love of the theatre came from her father, Alfred. He was a gregarious man, loving music and the theatre. He lost a lot of money collaborating with Henry James Byron, the dramatist, on the management of the Court Theatre, Liverpool. May first appeared in this theatre on stage at the age of sixteen unrehearsed, in the chorus-line playing the part of a sylph in the 'Mountain Sylph'. A year later, still in the chorus line, she made her first appearance on the London stage on April 11 1882 in the operetta 'La Mascotte'. After eighteen months, and still in the chorus line, May took steps to change direction. She wanted to be an actress and that would never happen while she was thus employed. She applied to the St. James Theatre for an audition and much to her surprise was given an interview.

May stayed at the St. James for two years understudying for the well-established actors, and in small parts while learning her craft. However she felt the days of playing the understudy had come to an end and it was time to strike out on her own. She was determined to become a leading actress. Her chance came when she joined a touring company and played two weeks in Edmonton, London, with short tours of the small halls. They did twelve plays and May took the lead in eleven of them in parts such as Lady Teazle, Lydia Languish and Kate, and with the plays 'The Shaughraun' and 'East Lyne'. She made a good impression as Susan Throssell in Barrie's, 'Quality Street' at the Vaudeville Theatre and was in constant demand in the West End, appearing in such successes as 'Trelawny of the Wells' and 'The Madras House'. May married Ben Webster in 1892, in London and they had one child, Margaret, born in New York City. Ben was from an acting background and educated at Stationers' School and King's College, Cambridge. He was a barrister but chose the theatre for his living, making his debut in 1887 in the play 'Clancarty'. Ben and May lived for years in a flat in Bedford Street, Covent Garden. Their London home was a meeting place for English and American actors and was always a refuge and a comfort for those in trouble.

May did not confine her energies to acting alone, and had many other interests. One of those was the Theatrical Ladies' Guild and her diary records attendance at a meeting as early as 1892. The organization had been formed to help all distressed members of the profession, actors, stagehands, wardrobe mistresses, in fact anyone in need. The organisation hated the word charity and abhorred red tape. It took care of children, paid doctors' bills, provided coal and blankets in winter, and dispensed such items as spectacles and dentures. May became a member of the committee and later was for many years Chairman.

She was drawn into other similar organizations including the Actors' Orphanage, with its famous annual garden party, and the Three Arts Club, with its equally renowned annual ball. May arranged innumerable Benefits, made vast quantities of appeals, and sat on many committees and invariably gravitated toward the Chair.

She was drawn into the Women's Suffrage movement and in 1908 attended a meeting to hear Mrs. Pankhurst who spoke about all the concerns May already had, including the struggle for women to enter the professions, to become qualified doctors, lawyers and teachers. Even in the theatre they were only recognized as actresses, but certainly not as stage managers, directors, nor managers. One woman to break through such taboos was Annie Horniman, a founder of the Abbey Theatre Dublin and of the Gaiety Theatre, Manchester. Margaret Webster in her biography, 'The Same Only Different' wrote:

> May, with her built-in Irish passion for being "agin" the government", found herself becoming eloquent in defense of women's rights. At last, one of her friends remarked jokingly: "Why, May, I believe you're a suffragette"! May paused, slightly astonished. "Why", she said, "I believe I am".

In Dublin, in 1899, May Whitty, played the leading part in a play by William Butler Yeats, 'Countess Cathleen'. Yeats attended the first night with Maud Gonne, a close friend of the playwright. May had been one of the leading lights of the British stage for nearly twenty-five years when she appeared in her first film, 'Enoch Arden', in 1914, but caring little for the experience she made only a few silent films. In 1918 the fifty-three year old May had the distinction of being the first actress to be created a Dame Commander of the British Empire in recognition of her above-and-beyond activities performing before the troops in World War I. May had a succession of

Broadway successes, and then she and Ben took themselves off to Hollywood to live there for the remainder of their lives. Some of the films May appeared in were:

"Little Minister" (1915) as Nanny Webster.
"Enoch Arden" (1915) in a supporting role.
"Keep Your Seats, Please" (1936) uncredited as a Dowager.

"Night Must Fall" (1937) as Mrs. Bramson, for which she received an Oscar nomination as Best Supporting Actress.
"Conquest" (1937) as Laetitia Bonaparte.

"The Thirteenth Chair" (1937) as Mme. Rosalie à Grange.
"I Met My Love Again" (1938) as Aunt William.
Hitchcock's "The Lady Vanishes" (1938) as Miss Froy, Governess and title character, in one of her best roles.

Dame May Whitty with David Niven in "Raffles" 1940

"Raffles" (1940) with David Niven and Olivia de Havilland, as Lady Kitty Melrose.
"A Bill of Divorcement" (1940) as Aunt Hester Fairfield.
"Return to Yesterday" (1940) as Mrs. Truscott.

"One Night in Lisbon" (1941) as Florence.
"Suspicion" (1941) as Mrs. Martha McLaidlaw.
"Mrs. Miniver" (1942) with Greer Garson, as Lady Beldon, for which she received her second Best Supporting Actress Oscar nomination.

"Thunder Birds" (1942) as Lady Stackhouse.
"Forever and a Day" (1943) as Mrs. Eustace (Lucy) Trimble.
"Crash Dive" (1943) as Grandmother.

"Stage Door Canteen" (1943) as Herself.
"Lassie Come Home" (1943) with Roddy McDowall, as Dally.
"Flesh and Fantasy" as Lady Pamela Hardwick.

"Madame Curie" (1943) as Madame Eugène Curie.
"Slightly Dangerous" (1943) as Baba.
"The Constant Nymph" (1943) as Lady Longborough.

"The White Cliffs of Dover" (1944) as Nanny.
"Gaslight" (1944) with Ingrid Bergman, as Miss Thwaites.
"My Name is Julia Ross" (1945) as Mrs. Hughes.

"Devotion" (1946) as Lady Thornton.
"This Time for Keeps" (1947) as Grandmother Cambaretti.
"Green Dolphin Street" (1947) as Mother Superior.

"If Winter Comes" (1947) as Mrs. Perch.
"The Sign of the Ram" (1948) as Clara Brastock.
"The Return of October" (1948) as Aunt Martha Grant, her last film role.

May's daughter Margaret Webster, born in New York City, was an American actress, producer and director. Margaret Webster tells the story of meeting Elizabeth Bowen, Dennis Johnson and Padraic Colum at a symposium in 1952, on 'The Irish Theatre':

Mr. Colum, they told me, was the self-effacing little man in the corner of the Faculty Lounge, where I was being given tea. I got myself introduced to him. I told him that I hated having to miss the symposium, but I was lecturing myself that evening. "I'm particularly interested", I said, "because my mother played 'The Countess Cathleen' in the special performance when Yeats and Lady Gregory inaugurated what afterward became the 'Abbey Theatre'. He was very faintly interested and asked her name. "May Whitty", I replied. He disapproved. "It's not an Irish name". I bristled somewhat. "There are records of the Whitty's in County Wexford in the twelfth century; sometimes sheriffs and sometimes horse thieves; but there!". "Oh", he answered, nonchalant but firm, "they may have come over with the Normans, but they're not Irish". I could hear the ghost of Michael James Whitty come screaming over the white-pillared portico calling upon his great-granddaughter to do something with fire and sword.

Ben Webster died in Los Angeles 26 February 1947. Dame May Whitty died the following year, 29 May 1948, also in Los Angeles.

Chapter 12

*C*atherine *W*alters (Skittles)

*W*riters have produced at least four Biographies of Catherine Walters, not to mention the many newspaper and magazine articles that have appeared since her death at the age of eighty-one in 1920. Catherine was born on the banks of the River Mersey in Henderson Street, in the Park Lane area of Liverpool. She was christened in St. Patrick's Church on 23 June 1839, in what was at that time, one of the poorest communities in of the town. Poor Irish people had been settling in this district for many decades, mainly after the 1798 rebellion in Ireland. The Church of St. Patrick's fell into a state of disrepair after many of the congregation moved to other parts of Liverpool. However in recent years it has been restored to its former glory.

Catherine's parents were Edward Walters and Mary Ann Fowler, but very little is known about their background except that her father was a low ranking customs officer who at some time served in the merchant navy. The family eventually settled on the Cheshire side of the River Mersey in Tranmere,

Birkenhead, where her father became an innkeeper. Some of the local sporting gentry who came for refreshment after the meeting of the local hounds gave Catherine the opportunity to learn about horsemanship, teaching her on the horse that her father bought for her. The local people soon noticed her riding ability and life was pleasant indeed.

The good life did not last for Catherine and her sisters after the death of their father. He had accumulated many debts and the children were sent back to Liverpool to their grandmother. Liverpool in those days offered a young woman without an education little or no chance of escaping from poverty. On reaching sixteen Catherine took a job in a tavern in Liverpool where part of her duties included setting up ninepins in the skittle alley and it was there that she became known as Skittles, a name that would stick by her for the rest of her life. However this did not stop her from captivating the hearts and minds of the aristocracy some years later.

Skittles was a very bright girl who had experienced a different way of life living amongst the green fields on the Cheshire side of the Mersey and when she reached seventeen she took herself to London. She was determined poverty would not enter her life again and with her intelligence, good looks and riding skills she was introduced one evening in 1861 to the owner of a prosperous livery-stable. Although he was captivated by her good looks, he had his mind on business when he offered her a job, Skittles was to act as a kind of advertisement by publicly putting his horses through their paces.

With her good looks and trim figure Skittles filled the bill to perfection. By now she was earning a reasonable living and it was not long before she was generally recognised not only for her skill as a horse breaker but also for her beauty. Her employer was well connected and she was given the chance to ride in Hyde Park, where the rich would promenade with their horses. Her social standing blossomed and men flocked about her. Soon she was seen in very fashionable haunts on the arms of wealthy suitors, and in the very best of restaurants, her pictures were in the windows of the very best photographers. Skittles began to sway feminine fashion and ladies soon took up the pork pie hat, which she designed for riding.

Many of them felt contempt tinged with envy towards Skittles but whatever their opinions of her, she was a first rate horsewoman. On one occasion she amazed everyone when she won a £100 bet by jumping over the railings in Hyde Park. At the Grand National Hunt Steeplechase in Newmarket Harborough, she cleared an 18-foot water jump, which had already claimed three victims among the competitors. Skittles was so skilful on horseback that crowds would turn up in Hyde Park to admire the Liverpool Irish beauty who had by now drawn the attention of the Marquis of Hartington, heir to the Duke of Devonshire. He had been amongst those who had, years before, come to the parlour of her father's inn in Cheshire. He had not remembered her but Skittles had remembered him. Their meeting came about through their horses colliding and throwing her to the ground and he fell for her charms and beauty. Soon Skittles was established in her own house in Mayfair with all the trimmings of high society with her horses, carriage and servants.

Skittles had hoped one day she would be the Duchess of Devonshire but it was not to be. She sold her Park Lane house and set up home in Paris, then travelled around Europe. Ten years later in 1872 on her return to London, she was delighted to find she was still a popular figure and younger people who had heard of her but never met her, wanted to make her acquaintance. Skittles rented houses in the most fashionable parts of London. She had gained respectability but she never forgot her poor family in Liverpool. She always looked after her younger sister Mary Ann and the rest of her family.

Skittles was a good hostess, her parties attracted many of the aristocracy including the Prince of Wales, and Mr. William Gladstone was another of her guests. Skittles continued to draw large crowds to Hyde Park, people would wait for hours in the hope that she would appear and entertain them with her horsemanship. Skittles never married but in middle age she chose the courtesy title of Mrs. Baillie and she had a great affection for the Honourable Gerald Saumarez whom she met while he was still at Eton; they remained friends throughout the rest of her life.

In later years Skittles sought comfort in her religion, she

lived alone except for one servant. Her only visitors were Gerald Saumarez, her Catholic Priest and a doctor. She loved nothing better than to go to Hyde Park on a fine day just to gaze on the scene of her old haunts and past glories. It was while she was out in her wheelchair that she had a stroke. Two days later the once little beauty who could charm the most high spirited horse to obey her every command was dead at the ripe old age of eighty-one in August 1920. Her faithful friend Gerard Saumarez saw to it that Skittles had her last wish and was laid to rest in the beautiful little burial-grounds of the Franciscan monastery at Crawley, Sussex.

Many years after her death, writers still find Catherine's life fascinating in many ways as she rose from a life of poverty, on the banks of the River Mersey, then using her beauty and skill in horse riding to seduce the male members of the aristocracy. Peter Jackson wrote:

> When I wrote recently a biography of Lord Hartington, the nineteenth-century Liberal politician, I referred only briefly to his love affair with the courtesan Catherine Walters ('Skittles'). The book was intended mainly as a political biography and at the time I was writing it the existing accounts of the affair were based largely on gossip and guesswork. The recent donation to the Chatsworth archives of over 200 letters from Hartington to Skittles has changed the situation, and I am grateful to the Duke of Devonshire for allowing me to quote from the correspondence, which provides a valuable insight into mid-Victorian social life, as well as an almost day-by-day account of an unexpectedly intense personal relationship.

Chapter 13

cﾉ𝒜gnes 𝒠lizabeth 𝒥ones

*W*hen you tread the steps down into the Lady Chapel of Liverpool's most beautiful, gothic Anglican Cathedral, you will see the face of an angel looking down on you from 'The Noble Women of the Staircase Window'. On a bright day with the light shining through the window, the face of Agnes Jones lights up and her eyes meet your gaze - you may feel she is looking into your inner thoughts.

Agnes Elizabeth Jones was born in Cambridge, November 10 1832. Her father was a Lieutenant Colonel, of the 12th Regiment, having been ordered there a few days previously. Agnes was a delicate child until she was nearly two years of age when she was taken to Ireland, the home of her grandparents and the birthplace of both her parents. Her father was born in Kildare 1795, and her mother, formerly Elizabeth Smyth, was born at Ardmore, Derry. Agnes spent part of her early childhood at Ardmore and later, the family settled at Fahan House on the banks of Lough Swilly. On 12 August 1837 the Jones family sailed with their father's regiment from Cork for Mauritius, spending six years there. In 1843 after her father's health broke down, they returned home to Fahan House, a small but lovely spot on the banks of Lough Swilly, Co. Donegal.

From an early age Agnes had become involved with the welfare of others less fortunate than herself. In particular the care of the elderly, the poor and sick people at Fahan. The area described by one of the Jones family was of a heaven of natural beauty, loved by Agnes.

We all became attached to this sweet home, but Agnes, especially, ever clung to it with the deepest affection. It lies nestled among trees at the foot of wild heath covered hills, the waters of the blue lake rippling up to the edge of the lawn and then stretching out to the grey hills at the other side. Every variety of scenery is combined in the little nook, bare rocky-mountains which seem to bid defiance to the advance of cultivation, subsiding at their base into sunny fields or soft stretches of waving flax. Wooded park-like domains and bleak stony patches, alternating on the banks of the lovely lough, so appropriately called 'The Lake of Shadows' while here and there the blue smoke rises from isolated cottages which dot the landscape all along the winding shore.

In January 1848, Agnes and her sister were sent to the Miss Ainsworths' School, at Avonbank, Stratford-on-Avon. The two sisters had suffered under the severity of their governess and were hoping for a more pleasant change in their new environment. Their new place of learning was a cheerful and admirably managed school. Commenting on Agnes, her sister Josephine wrote:

Her ardent affectionate nature was drawn out in warmest love to Miss Harriet Ainsworth, who perhaps never realized all the gratitude she had called forth in the enthusiastic young Irish girl, who now, for the first time, felt her powers brought into action and her efforts to please appreciated.

After two years and three months at the school Agnes and her sister returned to Ireland, on the death of their father on 19th March 1850. During the summer of that year, the family left their home at Fahan House for Dublin. Before leaving, Agnes and her sister met two ladies, a Miss Bellingham and Miss Mason who were engaged in missionary work among the Roman Catholics. In the summer of 1852, Agnes and her sister, together with two of her aunts, made a tour of Connemara and were excited by the scenery of the west. Agnes, was moved by the poor people of the area to such an extent her sister Josephine again wrote:

Her heart was drawn in ardent love to the poor but intelligent peasantry, many of whom are wholly ignorant of the English language and all of whom had been brought up in utter ignorance of the truth as it is in Jesus. We visited many of the schools and as the Bishop of Tuam, with a large body of clergy, was making a Confirmation tour at the time, we heard several examinations of the bright-faced children in the schools, whose answers astonished and delighted us.

The orphan nursery at Ballyconree especially interested Agnes and meeting her kind friends Miss Bellingham, and then Mrs. D'Arcy, the wife of the rector of Clifden and Miss Gore, was an additional pleasure. She would willingly have stayed behind us in the West to work for God with Miss Gore at Ballyconree, in that great field so wonderfully opened up for the labourer but duty called her away. It did seem as if her life-long desire for missionary work might some day find its realization in that sphere. She chose one school, which seemed in special need and for some years collected funds for the payment of the master. So brightly did she picture the delights of Connemara that a friend gave her the name of "the recluse of Clare Island" and often playfully asked her when she intended to migrate to the wilds of the Far West.

In 1853, at the age of twenty-one, Agnes spent some time with her sister and other members of her family in Bonn, Germany. She visited the Institution of Kaiserswerth, and hospitals and schools. Agnes with one of her aunts, spent a week at the Institution, and considered the training could be of use in Ireland. During this time Agnes was also influenced by the work of Florence Nightingale in the Crimea. In 1859 she took herself off to London and was introduced to her at St. Thomas's Hospital and they became good friends.

Agnes entered St. Thomas's Hospital in October 1862, as a Nightingale student nurse. Later she was to spend a term as superintendent of a small hospital in London. This was later to be followed by her appointment as superintendent of the Great Northern Hospital, London, during the years 1863-1864. Unknown to Agnes, at that time Mr. William Rathbone, a wealthy Liverpool merchant, approached the Select Vestry of the Liverpool, Brownlow Hill Workhouse and offered to put a trained nurse in the workhouse to replace the system of having the sick nursed by infirm female paupers. He said he would pay all the expenses of the new system for three years. The offer was accepted.

In August 1864, Agnes was requested to go to Liverpool to meet the committee and give her opinion on various debated points relative to the arrangements to be made for her staff. After the lonely journey from London, a carriage was waiting to drive Agnes from the station to the workhouse. The large black gates were opened and a man was waiting to conduct her to the Governor's house. After a long business interview she was shown the rooms she was eventually to occupy on the ground floor. They looked out on a small court and low wall and beyond this lay the fever hospital. The rooms were dingy, furnished with a horsehair sofa, chairs, tables and a stool but no ornaments of any kind. The dark colour of walls gave a look of gloom to the whole interior. Undaunted, she went with the governor to visit the rooms proposed for her nurses and also the wards, later commenting on the latter:

The beds are rather close together and the wards low but all appeared fairly ventilated. There seemed care for the patients too plus a few plants and flowers, 'Illustrated News' pictures on the walls and a "silent comforter" in each ward, not the utterly desolate look one often meets in such places. I feel at this moment, completely at home here and the nervous fear I had in looking forward to it all, seems to have left me. I went to bed very happy and with the kind of feeling that I had indeed adopted the work. Whatever doubts I might have had before, seeing the place had made me feel I shall love it and be of some use. I trust, if God blesses and helps me, to be of use to some of those poor lonely ones. I was awaiting them when Mrs. Cropper Snr. and Mrs. J. Brougham came in, bringing a basket of lovely flowers all arranged in a glass vase, only needing water. It gave such a homelike look to my room and the kind thoughtfulness of the gift made me feel again the good hand of my God upon me. They soon left and I had a long time to wait, so I sat down to read the Bible alone and engrossed my mind, so ready to dwell on the nervous dread of the next hour. The ordeal was passed and no small weight removed from my mind by getting the first interview over. I remained for two more days so as to become perfectly acquainted with the proposed arrangements and suggest a few alterations. I asked myself, shall I ever be able to meet the dreariness, the loneliness, the difficulties, jealousies, restraint, disappointments, isolation? In my own strength, no never and yet when I look back, I see how God has helped me, how in the darkest moment a something has come, sent by that loving Father, a little word, a letter, flowers, a something which has cheered me and told not only of the human love, but of that watchful heavenly Friend Who knew His weak child's need and answered her repining or fearing thought, by a message of mercy which bade her trust and not be afraid. I have many things to think of and plan. I fear the nurses having too much leisure. I know they cannot rightly employ it as a rule. Perhaps, with uneducated minds, too little is worse than too much work, responsibility too, weighs less on them. I am so glad I have been in the house, in everything I can now more realize my future position and its difficulties. But I have, as never before, a consciousness of power to bring sunshine to those poor creatures, as if I could, with God's blessing, make a little ray of hope and comfort sometimes enter their sad hearts.

Agnes returned to Liverpool in the spring of 1865 to take up her new post of Lady Superintendent. On her arrival, in order to brighten up her rooms and give a home like comfort and elegance to them, Mr. and Mrs. W. Rathbone and members of the Cropper family filled them with various articles of furniture. Agnes felt overwhelmed by the kindness and gifts from the Rathbone and Cropper families and, so touched by such kindness, Agnes recorded it in her journal:

I was so humbled I could have sunk to the earth, I suppose the feeling is partly pride, the extreme dislike and sensitiveness I have to any obligation. But all this makes me feel as if people expected so much of me, this repaying beforehand of what I am expected to be and to do and to which I may never attain. Supposing, what is quite possible, I turn out incapable of conducting the scheme and have to be replaced not for any fault, but merely for want of the necessary governing and organizing power. I shall feel like the originator of the South Sea Bubble, for allowing people to be deluded by false expectations. I should equally dislike any future testimonial, but I could bear it more patiently had I been at work and done something. I shall look round on my furniture as if each thing were an accusing ghost.

I now spend about three hours daily going my rounds of the wards, which does not give me long to each and as I have not yet assumed the reins, I cannot do anything, not even sit down to read to a patient. But I get a few words to most and I think already, many look for me. There is so much that is very sad, which one realizes more when inactive in the way of remedy, but I hope we shall be able to lessen many evils in time, slowly and gradually it must be.

I hear few complaints and have very few requests, these chiefly for paper and stamps to write to friends and I receive many respectful nods from my countrymen. There is one very large ward entirely of Roman Catholics and on my first visit I had so many questions to answer, "are you a Catholic?" etc. etc., as no other visitors are admitted. I see many in various directions, reading their Bibles and have met several who seem indeed to rejoice in them.

One bright little child especially, who is one mass of sores, always looks so happy and his large eyes dance with delight as he repeats hymns, etc. He speaks so imperfectly that I cannot ask him much, indeed my deafness makes me lose a great deal. There are many poor blacks here, one has died since I came, severe colds are so fatal to them. One man from Manila is dying and only one of the patients can understand his language. There are many idiots and old people in their dotage, one keeps a birch rod under his pillow which he daily presents to me, with a long speech, others cry if spoken to kindly. I feel daily more and more glad of the work in prospect, it is such a field of usefulness if God only Bless us in it and I feel He will do.

Few have had such a happy life as I have and it is happier every year. Today in one ward, lay a poor black man, the dews of death were on his face and his poor parched lips and gasping breath told the same tale. Oh! how, I longed to go and nurse him. I was able to say a few words to him of Jesus. He said he was so weak, but I told him how Jesus could tell the secret of the heart and accept the weakest longing. Oh! the loneliness of these sick beds. Oh! the many, many wants. How we shall need strength and hope and faith in God! Then the thought which every one repeats, that "nobody ever comes into a place like this but by their own fault", meaning idleness or sin. A hospital is sad enough, but a workhouse! It almost seems as if over so many of those beds, "no hope" must be written, with reference to this world, friendless and hopeless. If in this life only ye have hope, ye are all men most miserable. How we shall need the love of Christ to constrain us in our work, to be as He would have us be with those poor sufferers, not as man would have us! Today I was only in the medical wards. A Frenchman, who does not speak English, much enjoyed a talk. He so brightened up and made me such a French salute as I moved on. I gave him a paper for writing and he seemed quite joyous with the thought of the answer.

An Italian was much cheered by my telling him I knew Naples well. I was rather horror-struck to hear that a policeman goes every night through the wards to keep order.

The feeling remained, of the class of insubordinates one would have to control. How earnestly I desire they may be the better of our coming here! Six hundred patients dependent for comfort, on my staff and me!

During this interval of waiting for the beginning of her work and the arrival of her trained nurses, Agnes wrote to Mrs. Pennefather on May 11 1865.

Dearest Mrs. Pennefather

I sit down to answer yours at once, as I have time now which I may not have again for weeks, we have not yet begun. I have been living here nearly a month, but have weekly put off my staff, their rooms not being ready. We hope decidedly to begin on the 16th. I go daily to the wards to see the poor patients and I am on the spot when wanted about arrangements, this and preparing a lending library, is the extent of my work at present. I do not feel the time lost. I feel quite at home here now and am pretty much so in the wards, though not able to do anything, not being in office yet. It is more trying work, however, than if I felt something were doing. I see so much that needs a remedy and can only sometimes give a little hint how to make a sufferer easier, or do it myself. But the scenes of various kinds and many deaths are very sad and I feel very much the absolute prohibition to say a word to the Roman Catholics. My question about the separate wards for Protestants and Roman Catholics has been decided for me. One of the guardians, whom I asked, thought it would involve endless difficulties. Thank you so much for wishing to help me in it. I look often to you, on many points it seems as if I could ask no one else and your letters always help me so much, if only by their sympathy. It often seems strange that I, who have so little self-reliance and would like every step directed, am obliged to take such an independent position. And yet I have been so led on that I could not help it and I only trust I may be more and more led to look to the guidance of the Ever-present and All-wise Heavenly Friend. I really must apologize for this letter. I have written on, often interrupted and forgetting what I had said and so it has grown. My only excuse must be my deep feeling of longing for more labourers and wiser and better ones. I so deeply feel how few get training for that work which, of all work, needs it.

Brownlow Hill Workhouse

Agnes began work on the 18 May 1865 as the first trained nurse in any public institution in Liverpool. Brownlow Hill Workhouse was one of the biggest in the country, at times with over 3,500 people. In 1802 a fever hospital was built separate from the main body of the workhouse, because of the risk of contagious diseases (it was bigger than all the other Liverpool hospitals put together). At that time infectious disease was one of the great dangers in the workhouse community. Writing on the 4 February 1867, Agnes wrote:

> I sometimes wonder if there is a worse place on earth, but I never regret coming and I never wish to give it up.

Less than two years after beginning her work, the new nursing system that she devised was extended to the whole infirmary as a permanent arrangement, and her methods accepted by the rest of the country. Brownlow Hill Workhouse Hospital, gradually ceased to be a place where the poor died without care, and in misery. Agnes fell ill on the February 6 1868 and was found to be suffering from typhus fever. During the short illness, Florence Nightingale wrote to an aunt of Agnes. 'I look on hers as one of the most valuable lives in England in the present state of the poor law and workhouse nursing'. However Agnes never recovered from the fever and died in the early morning of 19 February 1868, at the early age of thirty-six.

The remains of Agnes Jones were taken back to Ireland, where her funeral took place at Fahan, Co. Donegal, a few miles from Derry City. She was buried in the family tomb in Fahan Churchyard to rest in the land she loved so well.

In June of that year, Florence Nightingale wrote:

> One woman has died, a woman, attractive and rich, and young and witty; yet a veiled and silent woman. Distinguished by no other genius but the divine genius working hard to train herself in order to train others to walk in the footsteps of Him who went about doing good. She died as she had lived, at her post, in one of the largest workhouse infirmaries in the kingdom. In less then three years she had reduced one of the most disorderly hospital populations in the world to something like Christian discipline such as the police themselves wondered at. She had disarmed all opposition and all sectarian zealotism; so that Roman Catholic and Unitarian, High Church, and Low Church all literally rose up and called her blessed.

William Rathbone erected a ten-foot high memorial to Agnes in the Liverpool Workhouse with inscriptions composed by Florence Nightingale and Bishop William Alexander of Derry. It was in the form of an Angel in white marble standing on a stone plinth, named 'The Angel of the Resurrection'. The memorial was the work of the great Italian sculptor Pietro Tenerani 1789-1869. He studied with both Canova and Thorvaldsen, two of the early masters of Italian Sculpture. Of his many works on classical and Christian subjects, the best include 'Psyche with Pandora's Box', 'Cupid and Venus', and 'Deposition from the Cross' a large relief in the Lateran, Rome.

He made the tomb of Pius VIII in St. Peter's Rome and a statue of Simon Bolivar, President of Colombia. When the Workhouse was finally demolished, the memorial was moved to Walton Hospital, in Liverpool. In 1989, it was again moved to the Oratory at Liverpool Cathedral.

On November 13 1932 a thanksgiving service was held at Liverpool Anglican Cathedral for the centenary commemorating two outstanding Irish Nurses, Catherine (Kitty) Wilkinson and Agnes Jones. Catherine Wilkinson came to prominence during the outbreak of cholera in Liverpool in 1832 and it was the centenary of the birth of Agnes in 1832. Nurses from London and other parts of the country attended the service, which was held in the nature of a national thanksgiving service. The work of the two women was seen to have been of great importance. William Rathbone was also identified with the work of both women and was instrumental in bringing Nurse Agnes Jones to Liverpool.

The people of Donegal and Derry held an Ecumenical service on the centenary of her burial, attended by the Church of Ireland and Roman Catholic Bishops of Derry, and the Presbyterian and Methodist Church Leaders. There were many doctors and nurses present at Fahan Churchyard for the open-air commemoration in 1968.

Since 1869 a lasting memorial, a tablet of Carrara marble, entitled 'Grief' in memory of Agnes Jones, is displayed in the chancel of the Church of Ireland, Fahan, Co. Donegal. Robert Kell, Derry, delivered this piece by Bishop William Alexander of Derry and the people of Fahan commissioned it. On the base of the monument is a tribute from the Bishop William Alexander of Derry.

Alone with Christ in this sequestered place,
Thy Sweet Soul learn'd its quietude of grace,
On sufferers waiting in this vale of ours,
Thy gifted hand was trained to finer powers,
Therefore, when Death, O Agnes! came to thee!
Not in the cool breath of our Silver sea,
But in the city hospital's hot ward,
A gentle worker for the gentle Lord,

Proudly as men heroic ashes claim,
We ask'd to have thy fever stricken frame,
And lay it in our grass, beside our foam,
Till Christ the Healer calls His healers home.

Her sister Josephine in, 'The memorials of Agnes Elizabeth Jones' gives a good description of the work of Agnes:

I believe that in Liverpool Workhouse Hospital, things were better managed than in any similar institutions. An active governor and efficient committee prevented wholesale starvation or cruelty. But no general inspection can secure against individual oppression where the old system of pauper nursing prevails. Mr. W Rathbone proposed at once to substitute for those ignorant and worse than useless women, trained paid nurses and nobly undertook to bear all the expense connected with the experiment for three years. By which time he believed the success of the scheme would have recommended it to the board of guardians and it would be adopted as the permanent system. As soon as he obtained the consent of the committee, he wrote to my sister, who was then, in the spring of 1864, at the Great Northern Hospital, asking her to undertake the post of lady superintendent of the proposed trained nurses. After much correspondence with Miss Nightingale and Mrs. Wardroper on the subject, she agreed to this proposal. The plan could not, however, be commenced for several months; many alterations were necessary to secure proper accommodation for the staff and the nurses themselves had to be found. Miss Nightingale, who entered most warmly into the project, arranged that twelve of the Nightingale Nurses trained at St. Thomas's Hospital be sent to Liverpool. No materials exist, either in letters or memoranda, which will allow me to give a history of the work, which Agnes attempted and accomplished in the Liverpool Workhouse. Her life there was too busy a one to allow time for much writing and her home letters dwelt on the little details which she knew would interest us and gave no idea of the greatness of her undertaking, or her plan of operation. The hope, therefore, entertained by those who, originally suggested the idea of this memoir, that some history of the results of her work, some suggestions as to the way in which it was conducted, some idea of the general organization might be obtained which would serve as a help to others treading in the same path, must be renounced. That she thought over the subject and formed very decided opinions as to the relative merits of different organizations and administrations, we know, but she never had time to express these on paper.

Her letters and her diary, both hastily written (for time was very precious during those three last years,) gave no idea of the immense work she organized, or of her practical ability and great business powers. It has even been thought and suggested, by one of those whose opinion I have great respect, that the deficiency which must arise because of this, is a reason why this memoir should not be published and that it will tend to lower the vague but yet high appreciation, which does exist in the minds of many, as to what she accomplished in the Liverpool Workhouse?

I trust that the existence of her work, recognized by all who take an interest in the subject of workhouse nursing, will obviate this danger. The memoir has been compiled, not for the benefit of poor-law boards and Boards of Guardians, but for Christian women, who, reading the story of her consistent walk in paths of no ordinary difficulty and moved by the example of unwavering devotion to her Heavenly Master's work, may go and do likewise.

On the 16 June 2000 'Ireland's Own' published the story of Agnes Elizabeth Jones, an Irish pioneering nurse. After reading the story, Mary Devlin and her sister Margaret McGrath, from Fahan, Co. Donegal, set about finding the resting-place of this pioneering nurse at Fahan churchyard. Margaret and Mary found the family tomb including Agnes covered in vegetation and the surrounding railings in a sorry state covered in rust. They promptly set about clearing the area to give a better view of the tomb and a metal plaque bearing the name of Agnes Elizabeth Jones. The Devlin sisters represent The Inishowen

Heritage Trust, of which Fr. Edward Doherty, owner of Fahan House since 1982, previous home of Agnes Jones, is President. This Trust is now setting up a memorial to Agnes Elizabeth Jones and having her grave as a focal point of remembrance. Not content with finding the resting-place of Agnes, the Devlin sisters, then set out for Liverpool where Agnes Jones put into practice her nursing skills on behalf of the poor of the town. Within a few days of arriving in Liverpool they had spread their net far and wide like good fishermen, to pull in some wonderful people to help them in their quest. They visited the Catholic Metropolitan Cathedral that stands on the site where Agnes carried out her good work with the assistance of other nurses whom she had taken with her to the 'Liverpool Workhouse Hospital'. They also visited the Liverpool Anglican Cathedral where a tribute is paid to Agnes in the 'Ladies of the Staircase Window' in the Lady Chapel. One of the highlights of the visit was the 'Angel of the Resurrection'. The Inishowen Heritage Trust aims to commission a bronze statue of Agnes Elizabeth Jones, to be placed in the grounds of Fahan House. "The Londonderry Sentinel" February 25 1868, reported:

Such lives are like the rainbow in the clouds—the assurance of hope—the hope that, be the times what they may, kindness and self-devotion shall never perish from the earth.

Then how does this quiet every day life-work contrast with the noisy flaunting zeal which characterizes some of our efforts. No parade. No show to call attention to her work. Simply the patient, unswerving performance of daily duty. Some of the noblest workers the world has ever known have been the quietest; so quiet that the world has known nothing about them until it has reaped the fruit of their labours. As in the olden time so it is even now—we entertain Angels unaware, and know not that they have been with us until they are gone, and we mark the void that is left by their departure.

*The Devlin sisters at
'Ladies of the Staircase Window' in the
Lady Chapel, Liverpool Anglican Cathedral*

*Agnes in the 'Ladies of the Staircase Window' in the
Lady Chapel, Liverpool Anglican Cathedral*

*'The Angel' memorial to Agnes in the Workhouse
Infirmary before the building was demolished in 1929.
The monument is now in the Oratory at the
Liverpool Anglican Cathedral*

*The former home of the Jones family, with the
author standing in the foreground. Agnes spent part
of her childhood in this house*

Chapter 14

Josephine Elizabeth Butler

'I was struck with the force of her mind, and I thought her perfectly and rather remarkably feminine'.
William Gladstone, British Prime Minister,

*J*osephine Butler is one of the many women in the nineteen century whose social conscience drove her to try to relieve the poverty of the poor in Liverpool and give them a better life. She was born on 13 April 1828 at Glendale Dilston, Northumberland, where her father, John Grey, was a political reformer and radical agricultural reformer and abolitionist, a strong advocate of social reform, and a campaigner against the slave trade. He was a cousin of Earl Grey, British Prime Minister between 1830-1834. One of seven children, Josephine was educated chiefly by her mother, a devout Moravian Christian, although she briefly attended school in Newcastle.

In 1852 she met George Butler, a lecturer at Durham University, and after their marriage in 1852 they lived in Oxford, where she suffered from the academic hypocrisy towards women. Later the Butlers moved to Cheltenham, where George was offered the post of Vice-President of the College. The move to Cheltenham did not make life any easier for Josephine and her husband as they had four children. In 1863, Eva, Josephine's only daughter, fell to her death in front of her at the age of 6 years. Josephine was devastated and never fully recovered from this family tragedy.

In the winter of 1865, George Butler received a hand delivered message from Mr. Parker, of Liverpool, asking him to accept the Principalship of the Liverpool College. It had been vacated on the retirement of Dr. Howson, when he became Dean of Chester. George went to Liverpool to see Mr. Parker, the Directors of the College, and others interviewing for the post of the new Principal. The Butlers moved to Liverpool in January 1866. In an attempt to cope with her grief, Josephine Butler became involved in charity work. This involved her visiting the local workhouse and rescuing young prostitutes from the streets. She wasted no time in trying to enlist people of influence when she wrote to the Lord Mayor of Liverpool:

Sir,

I thank you for the kind reception, which you gave to my letter addressed to you in March. I write once more to say that the generous promises of support which I have received encourage me to persevere in the effort which I described to you, and at the same time I wish to define more clearly what the class of women is which this work, with others, I hope, which may succeed it, is destined to benefit. It is the class of those who have not yet overstepped the line which separate innocence and guilt, but who, surrounded by a corrupt moral atmosphere and destitute of honest resources, are liable to become at any moment a passive burden on the public, or a positive plague - supported by the rates, or by theft, or by an alternative more shameful still. It is acknowledged that this class has not been sufficiently considered in Liverpool.

It is a common remark among those who are trying privately to succour the poor, that when a girl is simply in danger it is very difficult to offer her effectual help. For want of sufficient preventive agencies whose aid they may evoke charitable persons are sometimes actually obliged to wait till the man or woman whom they would fain assist has claimed the attention of the community by some overt act of crime or despair. The Matrons of several penitentiaries have told me that they have frequently to refuse applicants for admission because amidst all their wretchedness they have abstained from making a profession of vice. The Matrons add that it is much to be wished that such applicants could be directed to some Refuge of a more general kind.

In this town we have refuges for discharged prisoners, reformatories, penitentiaries and the like, which unite instruction and sternness, and render discipline instrumental to moral renovation and subsequent restitution to society. This a noble work, and there is a great need of all existing refuges for fallen women, there is a great need for more. But we must be aware that our charitable efforts on the one hand may be made to swell the inducements which the poor already have to do evil, unless they are balanced on the other hand by equally earned efforts on the behalf of those who, comparatively speaking at least, have resisted temptation. And while in London and in most towns, as much has been done for protection, as for rescue, in Liverpool this has not been the case.

If these destitute women do not become criminals they become paupers. For most of them the workhouse practically means the oakum-sheds, which, thus replenished, become a problem too difficult for the ablest and most benevolent of Workhouse Governors, and involves, as we have seen, a moral atmosphere and a type of occupation directly destructive of self-dependence and self-respect. The despondency of the pauper is the most sluggish of social sores.

But no argument is needed to enforce the economy of prevention, to show the advantages of a conception of charity, which aims at employing the experience and education of the higher classes to direct the energies of the lower, which comes from the head and the heart rather from the pocket. For indeed schemes like these, recently started, but surely spreading, have found more nearly self-supporting than any others, which strike as deeply at the roots of misery and crime. For the results are not such as political economists need fear. We shall not foster indolence by organising industry. The causes which have produced this mass of female destitution are not new, or peculiar to Liverpool.

Working women will obviously be worse off than working men if the proportion between the number of occupations open to women and the number of occupations open to men is less than the proportion between the number of women and the number of men seeking support from these occupations. And in point of fact almost everywhere, except in certain manufacturing centres, the number of openings offered to women has hitherto been not only absolutely but relatively smaller than the number of openings offered to men, and consequently the trades to which women are admitted have been almost always overstocked. There is no radical cure for this disproportion till men shall cease to consider sex as a disqualification per se for occupations for which women are practically fit. In the meantime the condition of the working woman, almost always worse than that of the working man, becomes very much worse when her disadvantages are aggravated by local circumstances.

Liverpool, the queen of seaports, shares the miseries as well as the glories of a people whose home is on the deep. Women here exceed men in number, and of these women an unusually large percentage have to support themselves. Sudden failures of dockyard employment, deaths at sea, and the virtual widowhood and orphanage of the families of many sailors who are not dead—causes like these leave unsupported many women who have married too young to have had any opportunity of learning a trade or practising for domestic service. It is mainly to such widows and orphans that I would offer an Industrial Home.

No doubt some of them have homes already. In No. 13, Robertson Street, says Dr Trench in his report on the health of Liverpool in 1866, seven adults and three children slept in a room of 594 cubic feet, and in No. 17 of the same street ten adults live in a room of 600 cubic feet. In No. 13 in 5 Court, Hawke Street, seven adults occupied a room of the same dimensions. The number of six adults in a room of 600 cubic feet is very common. In all cases where adults are spoken of, there is a mixture of sexes, and therefore an offence against moral and hygienic law. The contact of home influences is sometimes spoken of as a blessing to be preserved at any cost. Does this mean the physical, continuous, and compulsory contact of dissolute adults? Enough of horror but let no man think that I am proposing a work, which he can innocently leave undone.

Industrial Homes such as I desire to see established would not be, strictly speaking, Industrial Schools, for girls would not be received under sixteen years of age. But young women would be taught to work, subjected to a needful discipline, and at the same time exposed to elevating and religious influences, so that their moral and industrial training would go on at once.

Those whose hearts are warm in any matter are loath to think that they have said enough. But here I cannot bear to add any formal appeal. When the very stones cry out I need not interpret. Nor can I suppose that I speak to men unwilling to hear. Where the poison-weeds of crime and misery grow so rank I must believe that God has planted in many hearts their antidote, Pity.

I remain, Sir, yours faithfully,

Josephine E. Butler, 16, Parkfield Gardens, Toxteth Park, Liverpool. June 1 1867.

One of the leading merchant families who would have given Josephine moral and practical support would have been the Rathbones. William Rathbone V and his wife Elizabeth supported Kitty Wilkinson in her great work during the terrible cholera outbreak of 1832. William Rathbone VI was responsible for encouraging Nurse Agnes Jones to come to Liverpool in 1863. Josephine Butler took up the story once more when she wrote:

Liverpool is one of the largest seaports of the world. No greater contrast with this town could have been found, than the one presented to the academic, intellectual character of Oxford, or the quiet educational and social conditions at Cheltenham. Liverpool's immense population, with a large intermingling of foreign elements, its twelve miles of docks lined with warehouses, its magnificent shipping, its cargoes and foreign sailors from every part of the world and from every nation of the earth, its varieties in the way of creeds and places of worship, its great wealth and its abject poverty, the perpetual movement, the coming and going, and the clash of interests in its midst, these combined to make Liverpool a city of large and international character, and of plentiful opportunities for the exercise of public spirit and catholic sentiment.

The college shared the characteristics of the city in the midst of which it was set. Among its eight to nine hundred pupils, there were Greeks, Armenians, Jews, Chinese, Negroes, Americans, French, Germans, and Spaniards, as, well as Welsh, Irish, Scotch and English. These represented many different religious persuasions. A man of narrow theological views would scarcely have found the position as head of such a school agreeable. Firmness and simplicity of faith, truth, charity and toleration, were qualities which were needed in the administrator of such a little world of varied international and denominational elements.

The principalship must be held, according to the rules of the college, by a member of the Church of England, and the directors had been happy in finding churchmen who were willing to accept the conditions presented, and able to work well in the midst of them. There were, as pupils at the college, the sons of two half-civilised African Kings, Oko Jumbo and Jah-Jah. Their fathers, having been old and sworn enemies, the two little fellows began their school acquaintance with many a tussle true to the inherited instinct. They were good boys, however, and one of them afterwards a convinced and consistent Christian became a missionary among his own countrymen, in spite of much opposition and even persecution, it was said, from his own father.

When we came to Liverpool in 1866, and my husband and sons began their regular life at the College, going there early and returning in the evening, I was left many hours every day alone, empty-handed and sorrowful, the thought continually returning, "How sweet the presence of my little daughter would have been now". Most people, who have gone through any such experience, will understand me when I speak of the ebb and flow of sorrow. The wave retires perhaps after the first bitter weeks, and a kind of placid acquiescence follows.

It may be only a natural giving way of the power of prolonged resistance of pain. Then there comes sometimes a second wave, which has been silently gathering strength, holding back, so to speak, in order to advance again with all its devouring force, thundering upon the shore. But who can write the rationale of sorrow? And who can explain its mysteries, its apparent inconsistencies and unreasonableness, its weakness and its strength? I suffered much during the first months in our new home. Music, art, reading, all failed as resources to alleviate or to interest. I became possessed with an irresistible desire to go forth and find some pain keener than my own, to meet with people more unhappy than myself (for I knew there were thousands of such).

I did not exaggerate my own trial. I only knew that my heart ached night and day, and that the only solace possible would seem to be to find other hearts which ached night and day, and with more reason than mine. I had no clear idea beyond that, no plan for helping others, my sole wish was to plunge into the heart of some human misery, and to say (as I now knew I could) to afflicted people, "I understand: I too have suffered".

Liverpool during this period had more than its fair share of misery as hundreds of thousands of people entered the town in search of a better life by securing passage on ships for America. Among them were English, Scottish and Irish, Germans, Scandinavians. Between 1819 and 1859 four and half million Europeans sailed to the United States and half a million to Canada, two thirds of them through the port of

Liverpool. Not all of these sailed on, and Liverpool's population became increasingly cosmopolitan, with many nationalities making their home here. There was an immense workhouse containing at that time, five thousand people, and it was a little town within a town. Josephine Butler wrote:

> The general hospital for paupers included in it was blessed then by the angelic presence of Agnes Jones (whose work of beneficence was recorded after her death), but the other departments in the great building were not so well organised as they came to be some years later. There were extensive special wards, where unhappy girls drifted like autumn leaves when the winter approached, many of them to die of consumption, little cared for spiritually; for over this portion of the hospital Agnes Jones was not the presiding genius. There was on the ground floor a Bridewell for women, consisting of huge cellars, bare and unfurnished, with damp stone floors. These were called the "oakum sheds," and to these came voluntarily creatures driven by hunger, destitution, or vice, begging for a few nights' shelter and a piece of bread, in return for which they picked their allotted portion of oakum. Others were sent there as prisoners.

Josephine describes how she had to beg permission from the Select Vestry (administrators of the Workhouse) to be allowed to visit the women and young girls in the oakum sheds:

> I was taken into an immense gloomy vault filled with women and girls, more than two hundred probably at that time. I sat on the floor among them and picked oakum. They laughed at me, and told me my fingers were of no use for that work, which was true. But while we laughed we became friends. I proposed that they should learn a few verses to say to me on my next visit. I recollect a tall, dark, handsome girl standing up in our midst, among the damp refuse and lumps of tarred rope, and repeating without a mistake and in a not unmusical voice, clear and ringing, that wonderful fourteenth chapter of St. John's Gospel the words of Jesus

all through, ending with, "Peace I leave with you". The result of my visits to the hospital and quays and oakum sheds was to draw down upon my head an avalanche of miserable but grateful womanhood.

Such a concourse gathered round our home that I had to stop to take breath, and consider some means of escape from the dilemma by providing some practical help, moral and material. There were not at that time many enlightened missions or measures in the town for dealing with the refuse of society. There was the Catholic Refuge of the Good Shepherd, some way in the country, an old-fashioned Protestant Penitentiary, rather prison-like in character; another smaller refuge; and, best of all, a Home recently established by Mrs. Cropper.

But it must not be supposed that the majority of my oakum-shed friends were of a character to seek such asylums. Many of them and especially the Irish Catholics prided themselves on their virtue, and well they might, considering their miserable surroundings. Girls for the most part earned a scanty living by selling sand in the streets (for cleaning floors), or the refuse of the markets to the poorest of the population. Usually they were barefooted and bonnetless.

The Lancashire women are strong and bold. The criminals of the oakum sheds and prison, sent to "do a week" or a month there, had most frequently been convicted of fighting and brawling on the quays and docks, of theft or drunkenness. There was stuff among them to make a very powerful brigade of workers in any active good cause. But there were others the children of intemperate and criminal parents who were, humanly speaking, useless, not quite "all there," poor, limp, fibreless human weeds. These last were the worst of all to deal with.

I had the help at this time of a widowed sister who was visiting Liverpool, and who, in spite of very delicate health, threw herself heroically into the effort to help this work without a name, which came upon us. We had a dry cellar in our house and a garret or two these we crowded as many as possible of the most friendless girls who were anxious to make a fresh start. This became inconvenient, and so in time my husband and I ventured to take a house near our own, trusting to find funds to furnish and fill it with inmates. This was the "House of Rest," which continued for many years, and developed, about the time we left Liverpool, into an incurable hospital, supported by the town. It was there that, a little later, women incurably ill were brought from the hospitals or their wretched homes, their beds in hospital being naturally wanted for others.

A few months later, encouraged by the help offered by a number of generous Liverpool merchants and other friends. Josephine acquired a very large suitable house, with gardens, to serve as an industrial home for the healthy and active, barefooted sand girls, and other friendless waifs and strays. George Butler held a service for a gathering of friends and neighbours at its opening of the industrial home. Josephine said his dedication prayer on that occasion was very touching, and full of kindness and heart yearning towards the poor disinherited beings whom they desired to gather in.

The house was soon filled, and was successfully managed by a Matron, who was a mother herself. Besides the usual laundry and other work, Josephine set up a little envelope factory in one of the spacious rooms. This work required some skill, and this interested the girls very much. Several tradesmen and firms bought their envelopes at wholesale prices, and Josephine supplied some private friends who were disposed to help.

She also set up a House of Rest for Incurables; although some did recover, Josephine wrote:

> There was a very peaceful atmosphere in that house answering to its name a spirit of repose, contentment, and even gaiety among the young inmates, scarcely clouded even by the frequent deaths, which came generally as a happy and not unexpected release, and were regarded by the living as a series of fresh bonds between the family in heaven and that on earth.

Alcoholic abuse was always a problem with some of the girls in Josephine's care; she wrote: "Drink was the great, the hopeless obstacle which I found among them. It was on this side that they would lapse again and again. Though it involved no change in my own habits, I thought it was best to take the pledge. I joined the Good Templars, who had many lodges in Liverpool." Josephine was always very close to her family, recalling a visit by her sister when she wrote:

Shortly before the creation of these two homes, we had a visit from my sister, Madame Meuricoffre. She and her husband, with their dear little girl, Josephine, had come from Naples to England, and had paid a visit to our father in Northumberland. They had, a short time before, lost a beloved child, their little Beatrice, during an outbreak of cholera in Naples. The surviving little girl seemed to get worse after the death of her companion. She (little Josephine) took ill on the way from the North, and before they reached Liverpool this darling of her parents had gone to join her beloved sister in the presence of God. The parents came to us in deep sorrow, bringing with them the earthly remains of their child.

My sister joined me in my visits to the sick, criminal, and outcast women of Liverpool. We visited the wards of the great hospital together. The strong sympathy of her loving nature quickly won the hearts of desolate young girls, while she greatly strengthened me in the hope that we might be able to undo some of their heavy burdens. Among the first who came to us to our own house, to die, was a certain Marion, who seemed to us a kind of first-fruits of the harvest, in the gathering in of which we were to be allowed in after years to participate.

The first time I saw her was in a crowded room. She appeared to be in her late teens and her face attracted me, not beautiful in the common acceptation of the word, but having a power greater than beauty; eyes full of intelligence and penetration; a countenance at once thoughtful and frank, with at times a wildly seeking look, as if her whole being cried out, "Who will show us any good?" She was ill, her lungs fatally attacked. I went up to her, and with no introduction of myself said, "Will you come with me to my home and live with me? I had a daughter once."

She replied with a gasp of astonishment, grasping my hand as if she would never let it go again. I brought her home, my husband supported her upstairs, and we laid her on the couch in the pretty little spare room looking on the garden. She lived with us, an invalid, three months, and then died. It was difficult to suppress the thought, if she had not been so destroyed, what a brightness and blessing she might have been in the world. Untaught, unacquainted with the Scriptures till she came to us, she mastered the New Testament so thoroughly in that brief time that her acute questions and pregnant remarks were often a subject of wonder to my husband, who spent a portion of almost every evening with her in her room, conversing with and instructing her.

Some of the intellectual difficulties, which assail thoughtful students, occurred to her. I witnessed many a severe struggle in her mind. She would often say, "I will ask Mr. Butler about it this evening." But her questions were sometimes such as cannot be answered, except by God Himself to the individual soul. This she knew, and through many sleepless nights her murmured prayers were heard by her attendant, "preventing the night watches." My husband said her remarks concerning the nature of a true faith sometimes strikingly, resembled portions of the writings of a well-known modern philosophical thinker, which she had never read, for she had read nothing.

I speak of her intellect, but her heart was yet greater. What capacities for noble love, for the deepest friendship, had been trampled under foot in that dear soul? A well-known divine came to visit us, and hearing of our poor invalid, kindly offered to see and converse with her. My husband and I agreed that we would say nothing to our friend of Marion's past life, for we thought that, saintly man though he was, he probably had not faith enough to do justice to her and to himself in the interview if he had this knowledge. (There are few men whose faith comes up to that measure.) When he joined us again downstairs his face was radiant, and he spoke, not of any teaching or comfort, which he might have conveyed, to her, but of the help and privilege it was to himself to have held communion during a short half hour with a dying saint, so young, yet so enlightened, and so near to God.

I recall the day of her death. It was a cold, snowy day in March. In the morning my husband went to see her early, before going out to his college work. She could scarcely speak, but looking earnestly at him said, as if to reward him for all his painstaking instructions, and guessing what he wished to know, "Yes, God is with me, sir, I have perfect peace." Her long death-struggle lasting twelve hours, joined with the peace and even joy of her spirit, was very affecting. Though it was bitterly cold, she whispered, "Open the windows, for the love of God."

Her long black hair, thrust wildly back, was like the hair of a swimmer, dripping with water, so heavy were the death dews. She became blind, and her fine intelligent eyes wandered ever, with an appealing look, to whatever part of the room she thought I was in. Towards sunset she murmured, "Oh, come quickly, Lord Jesus." During that long day she continually moved her arms like a swimmer, as if she felt herself sinking in deep waters. Then her poor little head fell forward, a long sigh escaped her parted lips, and at last I laid her down flat on her little bed. My husband and sons returned from college, and we all stood round her for a few minutes. She had become a household friend. She looked sweet and solemn then, her head drooping to one side, and with a worn-out look on the young frail face, but a look, too, of perfect peace.

Josephine worked in the Police Bridewell and established refuges for destitute and ill prostitutes. Ann Jemima Clough also drew her into the educational struggle, acting as President of the North of England Council for the Higher Education of Women. In 1869 she was persuaded to take the leadership of the Ladies' National Association in the campaign against the state regulation of prostitution under the Contagious Diseases Acts. She developed a new style of militant campaigning, by taking direct action at considerable physical risk to herself.

She also urged action on the Continent, visiting France, Italy and Switzerland. In Brussels in 1880 her exposure of under-age prostitution eventually prompted W.T. Stead's article in 1885 against the white slave trade. She was a founder member of the National Vigilance Association although she drew back from the social purity movements. After George Butler's death in Winchester in 1890, she returned to Northumberland. She published many pamphlets, articles and books, continuing to edit her own periodicals such as 'The Dawn and The Strom Bell'.

Josephine was so affected by events in Ireland she produced a paper entitled: 'Our Christianity Test by the Irish Question', published by T. Fisher Unwin. In questioning those who supported laws to deal with the Irish people, she wrote: "Having leisure and libraries, do our rulers ignorant of history, when I speak of the upper classes not let it be supposed that I fall into the error of thinking that they read". She also covers Cromwell's massacres of Drogheda and Wexford and the penal code and goes on to tell us that the Roman Catholics who formed three-quarters of the population of Ireland were excluded from voting as electors.

Her home in Liverpool is now the Josephine Butler Memorial House, lecture room at 34, Alexander Drive. Her independent views on Irish Home Rule, the Boer War, women's suffrage, slavery and other issues found public expression through her many books, pamphlets, periodical contributions and letters to the press. Josephine is still remembered today in Liverpool with great affection and she is depicted in the Ladies of the Staircase Window, in the Lady Chapel in Liverpool's Anglican Cathedral. Josephine also had a great love of Ireland and its people, during the famine of 1845-1849, and she witnessed the terrible suffering when she was seventeen:

> I can recollect being awakened in the early morning by a strange noise, like the croaking or chattering of many birds. Some of the voices were hoarse and almost extinguished by the faintness of famine; and on looking out of the window I recollect seeing the garden and the field in front of the house completely darkened by a population of men, women

and children, squatting in rags; uncovered skeleton limbs protruding everywhere from the wretched clothing, and clamorous, though faint, voices uplifted for food and in pathetic remonstrance against the inevitable delay in providing what was given them from the house every morning.

I recollect too, when walking through the lanes and villages, the strange morbid famine smell in the air, the sign of approaching death, even in those who were still dragging out a wretched existence. Sick and aged, little children, and women with child were alike thrust forth into the cold snows of winter, for the winters of 1846 and 1847 were exceptionally severe and, to prevent their return their cabins were levelled to the ground.

Josephine questioned why Irish industry was discouraged, and tells us about the "Patriot Martyrs, Molyneux, Swift and Lucas", who dared to speak up against the cruelties imposed on the people of Ireland. The Act of Union of 1801 and the loss of the Irish parliament and that, the Irish Bar was rich in talent, one of the first designs of the English government was to corrupt the Bar. Josephine goes on to tell us that Gratten had described America as the only hope of Ireland and the only refuge of the liberty of mankind.

She brings to mind the famines of 1810 and 1823 and how General Gordon during 1880 wrote to The Times Newspaper from Glengariff in County Cork: "I must from my own accounts and from my own observations. That the state of our fellow countrymen in the parts that I have named is worse than any people that I have seen in other parts of the world". Mr. Fox in his book, "Why Ireland Wants Home Rule", said of Gordon, that he gave away his money and clothes to the people of Glengarrif in 1880. William Gladstone's reaction to Josephine when they met in 1872 was:

Josephine was perhaps the greatest of all the great Victorian women, greater even than Florence Nightingale, for it was she alone among her contemporaries who appreciated the problem of women's place in society in its most fundamental terms. The relative obscurity in which her name is still shrouded is largely due to the fact that her fight was against prostitution, particularly against its regulation and control by Parliament.

She was a beautiful and gentle woman with passionate Christian beliefs and a searing conviction that in buying a woman's body a man was as much to blame as the woman who sold it, Josephine was horrified at the passing of the Contagious Diseases Acts which gave the police powers to arrest and examine any woman suspected of being a prostitute. To her, these powers denied women a basic right as human beings. Against her were the 'establishment' a male Parliament, the Church, the military, the brothel-keepers and their aristocratic clients, and the prevailing view that it was not nice to talk about such things.

Josephine's husband George Butler

With the support of her husband, later a canon of Winchester Cathedral, Josephine outfaced the lies and insults which were hurled at her, and lived to win her long battle in Britain, on the Continent and in India. Josephine died at Wooler, Northhumberland, December 30 1906.

Chapter 15

Anne Turner

*I*n an age when the state made little, if any, social care provision, it was to be the voluntary efforts of individuals and charitable groups that ensured the support for those who were disadvantaged. In the later years of Queen Victoria's reign, men like Dr Barnardo saved lives in London's East End, while others, less well known (such as the Turner family) applied their personal skills and resources to alleviate the suffering and misery of their fellow man. This brought hope to the lives of people in often desperate circumstances.

Jack London, the American author of 'People of The Abyss' tells the story of the poor in the East End of London in 1900 and how they would queue all day to try and get into the workhouse for the night and be given something to eat. He described the conditions in the institution as extremely poor because of the large numbers of people seeking shelter for the night. Jack London said he always had great admiration for the Salvation Army who ran the workhouse, because they appeared to be the only people trying to help the poor.

As the 'Second city of the Empire', Liverpool in the nineteenth century was a prosperous community, although it had more than its fair share of poverty. Many of the wealthy merchants, who had grown rich on the port's success, supported or founded various institutions in the region, turning some of their profits into practical help for the poor of the town.

The Turner Home is just such an example of local enterprise, founded upon care and commitment. Anne Turner was born 1820, her maiden name was Whitaker, and she was the wife of Charles Turner, Cotton Dealer, born 1803 who came to Liverpool as a young man from Yorkshire, and served Liverpool as a J.P., and a Member of Parliament, and was Chairman of numerous, notable companies and boards. The Turner family lived at Dingle Head, an area of the city close to the River Mersey bordering Toxteth Park, where the growing prosperity in Liverpool was seeing increased land development in what was to become the suburbs. Charles Turner was committed to charitable causes as well as local politics, he also held the post of Chairman of Liverpool's Port Authority. In 1875 Charles Turner died and within five years his only son died. The double tragedy of the bereaved Anne Turner caused her to seek a way of providing a memorial to her loved ones. She commissioned a life size marble sculpture of her late husband and son.

In April 1882 Anne Turner gave £40,000 with an endowment, to establish the 'Home for Incurables' on the Dingle Head Estate, to be named in memory of her late husband and son. The Home opened in 1884, with its own chapel, with high timber roof, aisles and perpendicular east window. The original aims of the Turner Home were to provide accommodation and residential care for chronically sick men and boys. In its early days there was some criticism of the Home because admission was confined to male incurables belonging to the Church of England and able to pay seven shillings per week. Because of these restrictions, half-a-dozen lonely and miserable inmates had a magnificent building all to themselves. Such exclusive rules were relaxed and the home was opened to all chronically sick or disabled men irrespective of race or religion. Many changes have taken place in the organisation, running and administration of the Home. Anne Turner died 10 August 1902.

Chapter 16

Hannah May Thom

*M*ary Hannah Rathbone who was born in 1817, the daughter of William Rathbone V and Elizabeth Gregg of Quarry Bank, Cheshire, May, as she became known was the second of six children. Her father, William V set up in partnership with his brother, Richard, as commission merchants in 1809, and was an active partner in the firm, later Rathbone Brothers, until his death. He was elected a Liberal councillor for Liverpool in 1835 and Mayor of Liverpool in 1837, and fought for many causes. A newspaper report on his death listed among them, 'Roman Catholic Emancipation', 'Parliamentary and Municipal Reform', 'Freedom of the West Indian slaves', the repeal of the 'Corn Laws', the 'Penny Postage Scheme', and the 'National Education', and he was an active supporter of the 'Municipal Reform Act of 1835'; he took a strong stand against bribery and other forms of corruption in municipal elections.

He worked with his wife, Elizabeth and Kitty Wilkinson to establish public baths and washhouses in Liverpool following the devastation of the cholera epidemic of 1832. He was committed to the provision of popular education, opening the Liverpool Corporation Schools to all sects so that children of any denomination could benefit from them, despite heated opposition. He was also responsible for the distribution of the New England relief fund for the Irish famine, 1846-1847. He numbered amongst his friends and correspondents, Father Theobald Mathew, Cambridge professor William Smyth, William Scoresby, the Arctic explorer and Joseph Blanco White.

Mary Hannah Rathbone married the Rev. John Hamilton Thom, on 2 January 1838, and it was the first marriage to be solemnized in Liverpool's Renshaw Street Unitarian Chapel. John Hamilton Thom was an eminent Unitarian minister and writer, born in Newry, Ireland, and educated in Belfast. He moved to Liverpool and became minister of the Ancient Chapel of Toxteth Park (Unitarian) in 1829, and in 1831 moved to the Renshaw Street Chapel. He was editor of 'The Christian Teacher' and 'The Prospective Review' and edited Blanco White's autobiography, 'The Life of Joseph Blanco White'. His own works include 'Laws of Life after the Mind of Christ' (1883 and 1886). His last public address was at the opening of the Liverpool Domestic Mission buildings in 1892.

The philanthropic ways of her parents had not gone unnoticed by Mary Hannah Thom, when she took on the post of 'Lady Superintendent of District Nurses' in Liverpool. Her greatest impact on nursing came about in the Vauxhall district of town. Historian, Margaret Donnelly, a former resident of the Holy Cross Parish, recalls her childhood in the area and how Hannah May Thom, as she had become known to the people of Vauxhall area, made a great impression on her and the whole community of Holy Cross when she wrote:

I can recall asking my mam and her telling me who the 'Lady of the Fountain' was. She told me the lady was an Angel sent to Holy Cross Parish to care and nurse the sick and destitute. Over a century ago, the parish was largely made up of Irish immigrants who had fled the awful famine. Hannah May Thom's kindness so moved the poor and the sick of Irish Catholics that after her death, they saved all their coppers (money), week in and week out, until they had enough to erect a fountain and statue in her honour.

Hannah May Thom, a non-Catholic, was a wealthy, well educated lady and was a member of the Rathbone family, one of the wealthiest in Liverpool. At that time they amassed a vast amount of wealth through commerce. After their own needs were met, (their Christian values of which they were noted for) they gave their surplus riches to the poor to improve their quality of life.

Although non-conformists, they saw all children as God's children and so they poured their energy, as well as their money into a wide range of charitable causes, one being the poor, sick and infirm parishioners of Holy Cross. Hannah May Rathbone married the Rev. Thom, a Unitarian Minister. He founded a non-sectarian charity, 'The Ministry of the Poor', which in turn helped the most deprived areas in the town of Liverpool. It was at this time Hannah May became aware of the terrible plight of the people of Holy Cross. Soon she was a familiar figure moving freely amongst the sick, and learning all the skills of a nurse. She tended high fevered victims, delivered babies into the world and comforted the dying.

She knew that there was a desperate need for trained nurses and midwives and so she then became superintendent of the 'Nurses Training School' where she and her team toiled in the squalor of overcrowded courts and cellars that were crawling with vermin.

As an educated and wealthy young woman, Hannah May Thom did not have to nurse the dying, the poor, filthy and diseased, because she was 'well born', but she felt it was her vocation to become a nurse. Another nurse who was attracting the headlines was Florence Nightingale who was in the thick of the Crimea War. Hannah May Thom had been nursing in the slums of downtown Liverpool for over twenty years before she died in 1872 at the age of 55.

It was the people of Holy Cross, who raised a water fountain with a figure of Hannah May on the top. It originally bore a simple but patently sincere inscription.

'This fountain was erected to the memory of Hannah May Thom, born November 24th 1817, died 1872, by the many friends in this neighbourhood whom she visited in sick and sorrow'.

In the course of time the monument was damaged and a decision was taken by leading members in the Holy Cross community to dismantle it for safe keeping, and to store it away in a confessional box in Holy Cross Church. In 1987, Fr. Connor Murphy and the parishioners of Holy Cross took a decision that the Hannah May Thom statue should be brought out of storage in the church where it had been for many years.

It was in a sorry state of repair and a decision was taken to have it restored to its former glory. The community organised themselves to raise the £300 for the cost of restoration. The city council granted permission for the monument to be relocated to the garden of Mazenod Court, a residential home for the elderly in the Vauxhall area, in a ceremony attended by the Rathbone family in honour of Hannah May, and the clergy of Holy Cross Church together with the community. Margaret Donnelly stated:

Without a doubt I am sure the new location would well have pleased that wonderful lady. We formed a Committee when I was organising the Pensioners' Club. The Priests wanted us to raise money to have her restored, as she had lost an arm and she needed a good clean up, and Fr. Mee, organised the finally restored fountain. It was also agreed to put her in the Garden at Mazenod Court, as she gave her life to the Elderly, and that is where she is today. R.S. Rathbone unveiled the restored fountain on Friday, 11 September 1987. The drinking fountain is no longer active, it consists of a shallow basin on a stem and on it is the Bronze Figure of Mary Hannah Thom.

Chapter 17

Felicia Dorothea Hemans

O! where the living waters flow
Along the radiant shore,
My soul, a wanderer here, shall know
The exile thirst no more!
And borne on eagle wings afar,
Free thought shall claim its dower,
From every sphere, from every star,
Glory and of power.

Hemans

*M*any literary experts believe the nineteenth-century poet and playwright, Felicia Hemans, to be the most widely read female poet of the English-speaking world throughout the nineteenth century and into the early twentieth. During her lifetime, she published twenty volumes of poetry and nearly 400 poems in magazines and annuals. She was reviewed favourably in her lifetime by the major periodicals and was compared to such greats as Byron, Keats, Shelley and Wordsworth.

Liverpool has been blessed with many outstanding women who have conducted their lives in pursuit of matters which they felt were important to them. Felicia Dorothea Browne was born, at 32 (now 118) Duke Street, Liverpool, on September 25 1793. Her father was George Browne, an Irish wine merchant and banker who was born in County Cork, and served as Imperial Tuscan Consul. Her mother, Felicity Wagner, was of mixed Italian and German heritage and the daughter of the Austrian and Tuscan Consul to Liverpool. She was the fifth of seven children. When Felicia Dorothea Browne, came into the world in 1793, the town was a thriving seaport, not the sort of environment to inspire a future outstanding poet.

Felicia was only 7 years of age when her father's business failed about 1800, as a result of the war between Britain and France, so the family moved to Gwrych, in North Wales, to an isolated Welsh seaside house, later moving again in 1809, to St. Asaph, North Wales and a landscape that could inspire a gentle observer of life. Felicia was a clever child who began to read at an early age, making use of a well-stocked family library. Her mother undertook the education of her gifted daughter, who read novels, poetry, and studied the piano and harp as well as grammar and modern languages.

According to her sister, Felicia could recite pages of poetry from her favourite authors, after one reading. When she was eleven or twelve she spent two successive winters in London,  where painters and sculptors inspired her. Her first book of poems dedicated to the Prince of Wales, was published in 1808 in Liverpool and London, and included, 'England and Spain, or Valour and Patriotism' and was a remarkable work from a fourteen year old, but sadly it received some harsh reviews.

This was a difficult beginning for a young poet, but her strength of character and determination to succeed overcame her early critics. Two of Felicia's brothers were serving under Sir John Moore in Spain in the 23rd Regiment (Royal Welsh Fusiliers). Also serving in Spain was an Irishman, Captain Alfred Hemans, whom she had briefly met when he visited the neighbourhood and her adolescent infatuation did not fade during his absence. On Captain Hemans' return in 1811, the relationship continued to develop. Her poem, 'England and Spain, or Valour and Patriotism', is long in heroic couplets, written to bolster British troops fighting in the Peninsular War and was probably inspired by her brothers in the Army, as were other patriotic poems.

1812 was an eventful year in many ways for Felicia. In March, Percy B. Shelley was attracted to Felicia and corresponded with her, but her mother found him dangerous and made her discontinue the correspondence. 'The Domestic Affections' and other Poems was published in 1812 and Sir Walter Scott published one of her poems in 'The Edinburgh Review', just before her marriage, aged 19, to Captain Hemans on 30th July at St. Asaph Cathedral. This happy event was marred some months later by the death of her father in Canada.

After a brief time in Daventry, Northamptonshire, where Captain Hemans was adjutant to the local militia, the Hemans returned to St. Asaph, where all but the first of their five sons were born. Felicia continued to write prolifically. Her style from this era is coloured by her reading of Byron. He was not displeased by her adoption of his style, and wrote to his publisher that 'The Restoration of the Works of Art to. Italy' (1816) was "a good poem" and that he planned to take it with him on his travels.

In 1818, Captain Hemans moved to Rome leaving behind his wife and sons, all under 6 years of age. There seems to have been a private agreement to separate, because Felicia never saw him again after that. Whatever the reason for the separation, they appear to have kept it a private matter. Captain Hemans spent the rest of his life abroad, and Felicia Hemans never visited him. Letters were exchanged, particularly regarding the children, but Felicia was left to support herself and her family as best she could. Felicia and the children continued to live with her mother in Wales. Her poem 'Modern Greece', about the Greek Revolution, published by John Murray, who printed 500 copies, was sold out in 1821. Murray agreed to split the profit of £50 with Felicia. She was lavishly praised in her lifetime and almost on a par with Byron in popularity. Her reputation grew and her work only went out of print after the First World War. Felicia's love of Wales was reflected most strongly in a collection of Welsh Melodies, which included a tribute to 'The Rock of Cader Idris', seat of poets. Jane Arron gives a good account of Felicia in her article, "Saxon, think not all is won".

When Hemans' Welsh patriotic verses were published in the 1821 in the volume 'Welsh Melodies', she was hailed by her contemporary Welsh audience as a 'poet for Wales', and made an honorary member of the Royal Cambrian Institution in acknowledgement of her role as a popularizer of Welsh national identity. By birth of mixed Irish, Italian and German ancestry, Hemans appears to have been gratified by this reception. According to her own testimony she regarded herself as a naturalised Welsh woman, having resided in North Wales since 1800, when her father's failed business necessitated a family retreat from Liverpool to Abergele in Denbighshire.

Cefn yr Ogof Pass, which loomed up immediately behind the Browns' new home, for centuries was a key battle site between the princes of Gwynedd in their strongholds in Aberffraw and Dolbadarn to the west and the invading armies of the Saxon, Norman and Plantagenet Kings of England, coming over Offa's Dyke to the east. According to the nineteenth-century Welsh historian, Jane Williams, "no spot in the Principality has been more thoroughly saturated with blood". This spot was Hemans' 'scene of writing' from 1800 to 1828, during which years she composed by far the major part of her writing.

At the time of the Browne family's arrival in Abergele, a revival of antiquarian interest in Celtic history, led in Wales by the recently established societies of the Cymmrodorion and Gwyneddigion, promoted a local enthusiasm for the old battle sites and their histories, in which Felicia, as a young woman, seems to have participated. As some of her verses in 'Welsh Melodies' are translations from Welsh-language originals, it would appear that she could also at least read, if not speak, Welsh. It is an old tradition of the Welsh bards that on the summit of the mountain Cader Idris there is an excavation resembling a couch, and that whoever should pass a night in that hollow, would be found in the morning, either dead in a state of frenzy, or endowed with the highest poetical inspiration.

The Rock of Cader Idris

I lay on that rock where the storms have their dwelling,
   The birthplace of phantoms, the home of the cloud;
Around it for ever deep music is swelling,
   The voice of the mountain-wind, solemn and loud.
'Twas a midnight of shadows all fitfully streaming,
   Of wild waves and breezes, that mingled their moan;
Of dim shrouded stars, as from gulfs faintly gleaming;
   And I met the dread gloom of its grandeur alone.
I lay there in silence a spirit came o'er me;
   Man's tongue hath no language to speak what I saw:
Things glorious, unearthly, pass'd floating before me,
   And my heart almost fainted with rapture and awe.
I view'd the dread beings around us that hover,
   Though veil'd by the mists of mortality's breath;
And I call'd upon darkness the vision to cover,
   For a strife was within me of madness and death.
I saw then the powers of the wind and the ocean,
   The rush of whose pinion bears onward the storms;
Like the sweep of the white-rolling wave was their motion,
   I felt their dim presence,–but knew not their forms!
I saw them the mighty of ages departed–
   The dead were around me that night on the hill:
From their eyes, as they pass'd, a cold radiance they darted,
   There was light on my soul, but my heart's blood was chill.
I saw what man looks on, and dies–but my spirit
   Was strong, and triumphantly lived through that hour;
And, as from the grave, I awoke to inherit
   A flame all immortal, a voice, and a power!
Day burst on that rock with the purple cloud crested,
   And high Cader Idris rejoiced in the sun;–
But O! what new glory all nature invested,
   When the sense which gives soul to her beauty was won!

Felicia was deeply distressed by her mother's death in January 1827 but it inspired 'Hymn by the Sick-bed of a Mother'. After her two eldest sons were sent to Rome to be with their father, she returned to Liverpool the following year, staying with a friend, Rose Lawrence. It was not a successful move as she thought the people of Liverpool were stupid and provincial and they thought she was uncommunicative and eccentric. She visited Scotland in 1828, staying with Sir Walter Scott.

She made several attempts at writing drama, none of which was successful. The only play to be performed, 'The Vespers of Palermo' (1823), failed dismally in its Covent Garden debut, despite having the Kembles managing and acting (Charles Kemble was the Manager of Covent Garden from 1817). A few months later it was produced in Edinburgh where it was well received when Sir Walter Scott wrote a prologue. Her second effort, 'De Chatillon, or The Crusaders', was also unsuccessful. In contrast, her poetry was popular and sold well and thanks to her work, Felicia Hemans was able to support herself and her children.

Publisher, John Murray, was no longer prepared to accept poems for publication after financial losses and Felicia was left with the task of finding another publisher. Blackwood in Edinburgh accepted her work for publication as did Cadell, a London publishing company, and Felicia's earnings were much improved between 1828-29. Blackwood published a second edition of 'The Forest Sanctuary' and agreed to advance her £150 against likely success. This new edition, published in 1829 contains her most famous poem Casabianca for the first time. The book was so successful that Blackwood from then on paid her £100 for her books of poems in advance.

From 1826 to 1832 these sold well in America and she profited handsomely from the American market. George Eliot praised her poem 'The Forest Sanctuary' as 'exquisite', while Sir Walter Scott, criticised her for being 'too poetical' and for having 'too many flowers and too little fruit'. Felicia confidently used a variety of metrical effects and narrative structures. She was an observer of the times she lived in, and much of her popular appeal lay in her ability to write emotional verses expressing the sentiments of her time.

Her memorials to George III and to Princess Charlotte, treat George III's madness, and emotional responses to the royal family, with considerable sensitivity. In many of her poems, Felicia responded to the concerns of women of her time by idealizing and romanticizing woman's role and relationships. Her portrayal of cultural ideals offered comfort and support to those who found them meaningful. She wrote 'To the New-Born' for the child of her eldest brother. Florence Nightingale copied her poem 'The Better Land' for a cousin. It touched on concerns, which were particularly significant at a time of high child and maternal mortality rates, and where survivors sought comfort in religious belief.

Felicia's strong support of family ideals was one reason why contemporaries accepted her in the roles of loving daughter and parent, and treated her separation from her husband sympathetically, as an unfortunate circumstance which reflected poorly on the Captain rather than on her. While a number of Felicia's poems indicate the attractions and rewards of creative work, and the desirability of intellectual powers, the same poems are often framed to suggest that love, strong familial relationships, and faith are ultimately more important and lasting than fame. This does not imply, however, that creativity and faith are necessarily opposed.

Both her juvenile poem 'Lines Written in the Memoirs of Elizabeth Smith' and 'Thoughts During Sickness: Intellectual Powers', were written late in life, describing genius and imagination as divine gifts, which will be regained and fulfilled in heavenly life.

Lines Written in the Memoirs of Elizabeth Smith

O THOU! whose pure, exalted mind,
Lives in this record, fair and bright;
O thou ! whose blameless life combined,
Soft female charms and grace refined,
With science and with light!
Celestial maid! whose spirit soar'd
Beyond this vale of tears;
Whose clear, enlighten'd eye explored

The lore of years !
Daughter of Heaven! if here, e'en here,
The wing of towering thought was thine:
If, on this dim and mundane sphere,
Fair truth illumed thy bright career,
With morning-star divine;
How must thy bless'd ethereal soul,
Now kindle in her noon-tide ray;
And hail, unfetter'd by control,
The Fount of Day!
E'en now, perhaps, thy seraph eyes
Undimm'd by doubt, nor veil'd by fear,
Behold a chain of wonders rise;
Gaze on the noon-beam of the skies,
Transcendent, pure, and clear!
E'en now, the fair, the good, the true,
From mortal sight conceal'd,
Bless in one blaze thy raptured view,
In light reveal'd!
If here, the lore of distant time,
And learning's flowers were all thine own;
How must thy mind ascend sublime,
Matured in heaven's empyreal clime,
To light's unclouded throne!
Perhaps, e'en now, thy kindling glance,
Each orb of living fire explores;
Darts o'er creation's wide expanse,
Admires–adores!
Oh! if that lightning-eye surveys
This dark and sublunary plain;
How must the wreath of human praise,
Fade, wither, vanish, in thy gaze,
So dim, so pale, so vain!
How, like a faint and shadowy dream,
Must quiver learning's brightest ray;
While on thine eyes, with lucid stream,
The sun of glory pours his beam,
Perfection's day!

Felicia spent most of her life with her family in Wales, rarely travelling. She read extensively, and sought inspiration and detail for her descriptions of Greece, Spain, and the new world, in the writings of other authors. Her work suffered from her restricted experience, as she relied too much on the impressions of others and often used stereotypic images. Still, she captured much of the ethos of her day in her poetry. Today her best-known poems are probably 'The Homes of England' and 'Casabianca' (better known as 'The Boy Stood on the Burning Deck').

Casabianca

The boy stood on the burning deck
Whence all but he had fled.
The flame that lit the battle's wreck
Shone round o'er the dead.

Yet beautiful and bright he stood
As born to rule the storm,
A creature of heroic blood
A proud, though childlike form.

The flames roll'd on he would
Not go without his father's word,
That father, faint in death below
His word no longer heard.

He called aloud "Say,Father, say
If not my task is done?"
He knew not that the chieftain lay
Unconscious of his son.

"Speak, Father!" once again he cried,
"If I may yet be gone!"
And but the booming shots replied,
And fast the flames roll'd on.

Upon his brow he felt their breath,
And in his waving hair,

And look'd from that lone post of death
In still, yet brave dispose.

And shouted but once more aloud,
"My Father! must I stay?"
While o'er him fast, through sail and shroud,
He wreathing fires made way.

They wrapt the ship in splendour wild,
They caught the flag on high,
And stream'd above the gallant chills,
Like banners in the sky.

There came a burst of thunder sound
He boy-oh! Where was he,
Ask of the winds that far around
With fragments strewed the sea!

With mast, and helm, and pennon fair,
That well had born their part,
But the noblest thing which perish'd there,
Was that young faithful heart!

Felicia does not appear to have included Ireland in her patriotic poems. Had she even given a thought about bestowing such greatness on Irish people in such poetical terms, in all probability the British establishment may have rejected them. On the other hand she may not have found favour with Irish people bringing them into the wider circle of Britishness, despite her mixed Irish blood. Her brother was the British Commissioner of Police in Ireland and part of his duties would have been to quell any showing of Irish patriotism. An article by Jane Arron stated:

> Nor did the historical heroes of Catholic Ireland find inclusion in Hemans's Great British fighting family. Irish freedom fighters are not registered in her roll-call of the great, which with hindsight was just as well, given that, after she finally left Wales in 1828, Hemans was to spend

her last years in the Dublin residence of her brother Lieutenant-Colonel George Browne, the then British Commissioner of Police in Ireland. As her brother was tasked with the repression and policing of any incipient contemporary uprisings against the British Crown in Ireland, it would have been curious, to say the least, had family loyalties compelled him to welcome to his home one who had espoused in her verse the cause of those rebels' predecessors. But Hemans's 'Fair Isle' is always singular, a Britannia without Ireland, and a Britannia which, moreover, after 1821, with British unity and its global supremacy apparently secularly established, she reverts to calling simply 'England'.

She has been accused by some of her critics of creating passionately jingoistic poems, 'The Name of England', for example:

The trumpet of the battle
    Hath a high and thrilling tone;

And the first deep gun of an ocean-fight
    Dread music all its own.

But a mightier power, my England!
    Is in that name of thine,

To strike the fire from every heart
    Along the banner'd line.

A thousand ancient mountains
    Its pealing note hath stirr'd,—

Sound on, and on, for evermore,
    O thou victorious word!

Felicia moved to 20 Dawson Street in Dublin in 1831, to be near one of her brothers. She died there, on 16 May 1835, at the age of 41. Her death was attributed to a weak heart, which may have been the common affliction of rheumatic fever. She is buried in the vaults of St. Ann's Church, Dawson Street, Dublin. There is a window dedicated to Felicia in the church and a plaque on the wall to her memory, and all visitors to the church are given a copy of Casabianca (The Boy Stood on The Burning Deck), together with a short biography of Felicia. Fellow Liverpudlian, William Roscoe, thought highly of her, as did Lord Byron, Countess Blessington and George Elliot who regarded her as a great poet.

She is sometimes criticised for her outspoken views on Liverpool and its people, but one can wonder whether she was right when she turned her attention to the gentle society of the town and wrote: "That it was, exclusively, under the dominion of an aristocracy of wealth".

In 2007, the parish of St. Ann's, Dublin, celebrated its tercentenary having been formed in 1707. The Mansion House, the Lord Mayor's house, just up the road, was built for a Joshua Dawson, a merchant, in 1705, and he gave the site for erecting the church and vicarage house in 1707.

Isaac Wills, a freeman of Dublin, and one of the greatest architects of the time, designed the church which was built in the reign of Queen Anne, and was dedicated to St. Ann, mother of the Virgin Mary.

Painting of St. Ann's Church, Dublin

This Church is a proud possessor of a memorial tablet in memory of Felicia Hemans, and the poem on the memorial reads:

"Calm on the bosom of thy God, fair spirit! Rest thee now, e'en while the dust thy footsteps trod his seal was on thy brow. Dust to its narrow house beneath, soul to its place on high, they that have seen thy look in death no more may fear to die."

Read before the Historic Society of Lancashire and Cheshire, December 5 1896. The Liverpool Homes of Mrs. Hemans.

It must ever be regretted that the Historic Society of Lancashire and Cheshire did not undertake, at the commencement of its work in 1848, the identification of those houses in Liverpool and the immediate neighbourhood, which have been either the birthplaces or residences of distinguished people. It is inexplicable that no organized action was taken until 1892, when, on the suggestion of Mr. Baron L. Benas, the Council of the Society appointed a committee to inquire into the matter. Much may even now be done, but half-a-century too great a delay, particularly in a town where property changed so rapidly as in Liverpool. During the fifty years that have passed since the formation of this Society, the property in our town has been completely changed, the tremendous development of trade rendering necessary the alteration of what were once residences into business premises. Where, in the process of alteration, the houses have not been entirely swept away, the transformation in many cases has been so great as to render identification almost impossible. Of the houses with which hearsay associates the names of distinguished persons it is extremely difficult to discover anything to confirm the statements; and it is certainly irritating to realize that information, which in 1848 was probably considered too common to be worth recording, was unobtainable in 1896.

Liverpool Courier, January 21 1899 reported;

A very interesting ceremony took place yesterday in Duke Street. At No. 118 of that street (a few doors from

Kent Street on the south side) Mrs. Hemans (née Brown) was born on September 25 1793 and on the front wall a tablet has been fixed by the Historic Society of Lancashire and Cheshire recording the fact. The Right Hon. the Lord Mayor of Liverpool unveiled it yesterday in presence of a few members of the society and a small gathering drawn more from the accidental passers-by than from the admirers of the poetess. The Lord Mayor was accompanied by the Lady Mayoress, and among those present were Mr. J. Paul Kylaudj, F.S. A., vice-president, and the following members of the Council of the Historic Society: Messrs. A. M. Robinson, W. F. Price, G. S. Prentice, W. E. Gregson, H. Peet, F.S. A., E. Cox, W. F. Irvine, T. Goffuy, and G. T. Shaw (Hon. Secretary of the Tablets Committee), B. L. Benas, W. H. Picton, G. Atkin, Mackenzie Bell, and W. King

Mr. Rylands, in asking the Lord Mayor to perform the simple ceremony, stated that this was the first of a series of tablets the society were about to erect and that the next one would be put on the house in Rodney Street in which Mr. Gladstone was born. Some difficulty was felt as to the exact house in which Mrs. Hemans was born, but Mr. Shaw had satisfactorily solved that question, and Mr. Richard Roberts, the owner and occupier, kindly allowed that tablet to be fixed on the wall. This was designed by Mr. Price, and carried out by the Delia Robbia Company, Birkenhead. The Lord Mayor said that one of the most marked evidences of decay in character was the loss of that esteem and respect which was naturally felt for the great and good who had passed away, and one of the most striking illustrations of the vigour and virility of a community was that every opportunity was seized to express admiration and esteem for each man and woman and to imitate their high qualities and lofty examples.

No apology was needed for the selection of the beautiful poetess, Mrs. Hemans, for this honour. He was familiar with her works in his early days. She was projected on the imagination of the youth of his day as more modern poets were upon the youth of today, and although time and changes in the mental conditions of the people had contributed somewhat to place her works in the shadow, he believed there would be a day of resurrection when, in times of less feverishness of competition and less urgency in life's battle, these quieter muses would reappear on the mental horizon and Mrs. Hemans, in common with several others now almost lost in obscurity, would brighten the minds of those who followed the present generation.

Felicia was the personal friend of some of the greatest minds of her day, Sir Walter Scott and Wordsworth.

Her poems were favourably criticised by that prince of critics, Lord Jeffrey, and she won the admiration of Whately, Archbishop of Dublin, one of the strongest and most original men of his time. Wordsworth on the occasion of her early death said:

Mourn for that Holy Spirit
Sweet as the spring, as ocean deep,
For her who ere her summer faded
Has sunk into breathless sleep.

Chapter 18

Kitty Wilkinson

*W*hen Kitty Wilkinson came into this world in Ireland in 1785 she was christened Catherine Seaward. One can only speculate that on the day of their departure from Derry, the Seaward family must have had mixed feelings, leaving their home in 1794 to sail to Liverpool. News would no doubt have reached them that Liverpool was a rapidly expanding town, which would give them an opportunity to create a better future for their young family. A man would need a stout heart to take them on a sea voyage of over two hundred miles in 1794, but Liverpool it had to be.

The Seawards set sail on a winter morning in early February when the sun was rising. Catherine and her younger brother were exploring the workings of this small sailing ship while her mother sat cradling her infant child. Mr. Seaward paid more attention to Catherine and her brother to make sure they kept out of the way of the ship's crew. A more pleasant day the family could not have wished for, it was a bright morning and everybody was thankful for a few hours of sunshine. A seagull was perched on top of the main mast and appeared to be looking down at the passengers below, and then it spread its wings and headed back towards the mainland. The ship was making good time under full sail with a crew capable of harnessing the wind.

As the evening closed in, the Seawards and the rest of the poorer passengers on deck fell silent. The flapping of the sails against a soft breeze could be heard in tune with the rest of the ship's rigging. Vibrations and creaking deck planking sent forth a steady rhythm. The slapping of the sea against the ship's bow and the steady surge of the ship made up this orchestral performance of tranquillity.

As the night moved on the Seaward children became restless but this was not a problem to their parents. They had packed a good store of food and water, enough to last the journey's end, which had a calming effect on Catherine and the younger children. By midnight most of the passengers lying about the deck had settled down to await the early morn. It was a long night sitting for the Seaward family and the rest of the deck passengers. The ship's bos'un could be heard giving orders to the members of the crew still on watch although his voice had lost some of the power that it had during the daylight hours.

The noise of the ship's rigging seemed to grow louder because it did have to compete with the sounds of excited passengers. The sails took on a different colour as the dawn broke stirring some of the deck passengers from their slumber. Once again the sun was rising giving off its warm rays as ahead lay England, which had just come into sight of the observant onlookers. Then without warning the bright blue sky gave way to darkening clouds and this small sailing ship was being tossed about. The rain followed, and light drops were soon swallowed up by the dry sails and deck planking. The wind followed growing with intensity and parents gathered their children into their arms and a frightening silence befell the once happy passengers.

The ship's crew was doing its best to keep a steady course as they came into Liverpool Bay from the Irish sea but they felt it was a battle already lost. The rain was lashing against the sails as the crew tried to bring them under control and the sky grew darker. The ship's Master was fearful that they would be carried onto the sandbanks that lay on each side of the narrow channel, which led to the River Mersey. By this time screams could be heard from the frightened passengers in the cabins and those on deck tried to hold onto their children in the howling wind and rain.

The gale increasing its pressure on the small ship snapped the main mast sending it across the deck. The ship started to list to starboard taking it towards the Wirral Peninsula and away from the entrance to the Mersey. People on the shore across the bay at Formby could see the floundering ship. The crew of the only lifeboat, in the area, stationed at Formby Point, put to sea in the raging gale. It was no more than a large rowing boat fighting heavy seas to get to the stricken ship. By the time they reached her it had been driven further to the west and came to rest on the treacherous Hoyle Bank at the entrance to the River Dee.

Catherine and the rest of her family were holding on for dear life with the rest of the passengers and ship's crew. The heavy seas soon broke the back of this small sailing ship and she was starting to sink when the lifeboat reached her. Catherine and her mother and the two younger children were taken onto the lifeboat but there was no trace of her father. However, the danger was not yet over for the rest of the Seaward family, and Mrs Seaward was holding her infant child in her arms as the lifeboat was fighting its way back to the nearest shore. Then without any warning the gale force wind snatched the baby from her to be washed overboard. It is uncertain as to what happened to Kitty's father during that terrible storm. It is possible that in trying to save the lives of his wife and children, he perished on the stricken ship.

It is not hard to imagine the suffering of Mrs. Seaward finding herself in a strange town with two children and no home. They were not the sort of family to leave their home in Derry with three young children on the off-chance of finding work and a place to stay and it was doubtful that they could have been persuaded to leave their homeland on a chance that they might better themselves. Mr. Seaward was skilled and literate so he probably had a position lined up before he left home with his family.

After their ordeal was over Mrs. Seaward settled in Denison Street together with Kitty and her younger brother in the north end of the town. Denison Street was still occupied by professional and trades people during the 1790s and they rented out their cellars to the poor of the town. The whole of the area north of Liverpool was unspoilt during Kitty's early years. As far as the eye could see there were fields and meadows; the people who lived along the banks of the Mersey worked the land. After settling in, Mrs. Seaward soon found work for herself and Kitty. They were employed by a Mrs. Lightbody to do domestic work. However it was not long before Mrs. Lightbody realised that Mrs Seaward had more to offer and gave her the job of teaching the servants and other employees how to spin and make lace.

After two years in this employment Kitty's mother's health broke down and the family finished up in the 'Liverpool Workhouse'. Kitty by this time was eleven years old and those in charge at the workhouse had the right to transport children from an early age to a cotton mill. This could be done without the parents' consent because they were a burden on the Parish. Kitty had to sign indentures binding her to this new employer for ten years until the age of twenty-one.

She was sent to Low Mill in the village of Caton, near Lancaster, which commanded a view of the Lune Valley, and is still a place of rare beauty bordering on the Forest of Bowland. A treasured feature of the village was the ancient oak tree with the stepped stones shaded beneath it. This tree is reputed to be a thousand years old, and tradition has it that monks displayed their Lune fish catches for sale on the stones beneath it. During the 1790s most of the "apprentices" employed at Low Mill were recruited from workhouses in the Lancashire and Yorkshire areas and some even as far away as London, a practice widely used by mill owners in Lancashire, Yorkshire and Cheshire.

When Kitty reached her 21st birthday in 1807 she was released from Caton Mill and returned to Liverpool. On arriving there, her first task was to acquire suitable accommodation for her mother from the workhouse and herself. This proved to be no easy matter, as every available space was being taken up by those seeking to build a new life in the town. Kitty tried to find a place to live in Denison Street so that once again, her mother could be near old friends and neighbours, but there was no accommodation there. So they settled in Frederick Street in the south end of the town. Once the roof over her head was secure, her next task was to find work. Although Kitty was a bright young woman, she was not in a position to be choosey. The town had changed out of proportion to the one she had left when she was eleven. Liverpool was not an orderly town, unlike the village she had left, but it was an exciting place.

Kitty had the ability to present herself in the most effective way and it was not long before she found employment with Colonel Maxwell's family as a domestic servant. Mrs. Maxwell had taken a liking to Kitty after speaking to people who attended the same Church and spoke highly of her. She was very happy in her new job, and no longer had to suffer the long hours and the noise of the machines at Low Mill.

Although Kitty had to work hard this did not deter her and at last she was in control of her own destiny. When she was not on duty Kitty began to explore the town, and make friends while attending the services at her local Unitarian Church. It is almost certain Kitty had to sit on wooden benches at the rear of the church reserved for poor people in the community. However, Kitty would have been noticed attending church services by those in a position of privilege in the town, as she was a confident and proud young woman who would hold her head high.

The Maxwells proved to be good employers to Kitty, but she was only there for one year when they had they to leave Liverpool. Before they left, Mrs. Maxwell tried to persuade Kitty to go with them, but to no avail, as she was not prepared to leave her mother. Because of her ability and good work record, it was not long before she once again found employment with the family of Mrs. Richard Heywood, again as a domestic servant. This new post lasted for three years, when Kitty was twenty-five and she could no longer leave her mother on her own during the day. In order to look after her, Kitty opened a school where she could make a living for them both. She managed to obtain a large room, which served as her home and school, for five pounds a year rent.

In one corner of the room Kitty had a bed for herself and her mother, and her pupils took up the rest of the space during the day. Up to ninety children attended classes daily and sat on the bare floor. Those numbers may seem excessive, with so many children in one room, but if you were poor you had little choice and this applied to Kitty as well as her pupils.

Kitty did not need any teaching experience, the main considerations were premises and an ability to read and write. In those days a licence was not needed to start a school, compulsory education was still a long way off. This state of affairs unfortunately attracted unscrupulous people who had little or no interest in the welfare of the children, their main aim being to make money from the venture. However, whilst Kitty needed to make a living for her mother and herself, the welfare of the children came first. She had seen how children were treated in the mills and that left a profound effect on her. Those in better circumstances in the town rented their basements to as many as twenty or thirty people, without cooking facilities or water.

Kitty charged her scholars three pence a week. She taught them reading, writing and sewing, while her mother employed herself in making lace. At night when the school day was over, Kitty would go out and sell the items of lace her mother had made. Although the school was a success, life for Kitty and her mother was still very hard and at times it was difficult for them to afford food for themselves. No matter how bad things were for Kitty she retained a very happy disposition and always transmitted that happiness to her pupils, as she was a ray of hope and inspired her young charges.

The health of her mother was still a great worry to Kitty and as the months went by she became more of a problem including the times when her pupils were in class, as she was beginning to become confused. Whenever Kitty was away from their home, her mother would sometimes burn their store of food or destroy valuables and bedding. The neighbours would intervene in Kitty's absence, to stop her mother from hurting herself. In the middle of the night Mrs. Seaward would sometimes wander away to another part of the town where she had formerly lived. Her increasing violence frightened the children and caused Kitty to give up her teaching, which was a bitter blow. What she wanted most was to be in her little school passing on skills she had learned during childhood.

Kitty still had to make a living, rent still had to be paid, but it was not possible for her to go back into domestic work because of the condition of her mother. Kitty was prepared to do almost anything to keep a roof over their heads and would not allow pride to get in the way of earning money no matter how menial a job.

It was not unusual to see people in those days shovelling horse manure into buckets from the streets to be sold to farmers. The countryside, being so close to the town, also drew people into fields and country lanes to collect horse and cattle manure. Kitty, like so many desperate people in those days, arose from her bed at two o'clock in the morning to go out into the country. Armed with her bucket and shovel, she would spend hours collecting manure, then would leave this in a hole in a field for safe keeping, to be sold to a local farmer later in the day.

Kitty had to give up the room she rented, and found a place to live in the countryside away from the stench of the town where she hoped the fresh air would be good for her mother's health. However Kitty's employment prospects did not improve, so they had to return to town.

This time they were successful in finding accommodation in Denison Street, although it was only a cellar. This was the place Kitty's mother often wandered back to. Kitty hoped by going to live there, her mother might become more settled. Next door there lived an elderly woman alone who was a former friend of Mrs. Seaward. Kitty had often visited the woman in her cellar, which resembled a dungeon rather than a home. Several of Kitty's old scholars followed her to her new home, which was so small she could only accommodate a few children. To supplement her small income she would work muslin for the shops, a plain-weave cotton fabric.

The hard work was taking its toll on Kitty and her youth was quickly passing by. Then, at the age of twenty-seven, she met Emanuel Demontee, a French Catholic seaman. How Kitty came to meet him we may never be sure. However just across the road from Denison Street was the Borough Gaol, known as the French Prison. This was the main holding centre for French prisoners of war in Liverpool during 1800-1801, and Dr James Currie became very concerned for the welfare of the French prisoners. Many had died through overcrowding and the poor quality of the small amount of food allocated to them each week.

Other leading members of Liverpool's society took up the cause of the prisoners and agreement was reached with the French Government that the prisoners of war would be allowed to work in the community. In this way they would be able to feed and clothe themselves much better. It is possible that Emanuel Demontee was one of those prisoners and Kitty met him whilst working in the community.

They were married in the Parish Church of St. Peter, Liverpool, on the 5th October 1812. An observer at the time of the marriage commenting on the character of Demontee said: "By all accounts he was a very respectable man, and a kind and affectionate husband, and he agreed to Kitty's stipulations, that she was never to be asked to change her religion or the place of her worship, and her children if any, were to be brought up as Protestants." In 1812 long before Catholic Emancipation in 1829 it was not popular to be a Catholic, yet Kitty chose to marry Emanuel Demontee.

In 1813 Kitty gave birth to her first child, a son, whom she called John. Her second son Joseph was born in 1815 when Emanuel Demontee is reported to have been at sea in the merchant service. Kitty was in her thirties, but she learned her husband had drowned at sea before the birth of his second son. Herbert R. Rathbone in his edited memoir wrote:

> The young widow with two young children and an ailing mother to care for and her youngest child in poor health, was now trapped in a sea of misery once again, and having to face the fear of poverty. Her friends urged her to place

her mother in an asylum, but Kitty was not prepared to turn her back on her mother. Although Kitty had what seemed insurmountable problems, she had also concerned herself in trying to keep orphan children from the community out of the workhouse.

Kitty may have been trapped, living in cellars in the most appalling conditions; but her spirit was indomitable. She carried on fighting for her very existence, and yet she still had time for other people. Midwives were unknown at this time and medical facilities in general were very poor. However Kitty was earning a reputation for attending the sick in her area. Despite her ability to look after other people Kitty was forced to take whatever work came her way. She could not enter domestic service because of her children and her mother and needed work that would allow her to be home at lunchtime and to finish work at a reasonable hour in the evening. She found employment in a nail factory close to her home, which enabled her to see to her children and mother during the midday break.

The work was hard and the wages small, Kitty got three pence for every twelve hundred nails she produced. The average wage that could be earned was four shillings a week, but at times she actually managed to earn as much as eight shillings. Kitty paid the price for her hard work, her fingers were continually burned with the heat of the nails. When her hands were too blistered and sore, she would have to stay at home without pay and dress them until they healed again. After enduring this hard labour for more than a year she was forced to give up, in order to keep her sanity and general health. Not long after this soul-destroying job, Kitty, proud and strong as she most certainly was, was forced to apply to the parish for help in the maintenance of her two children and mother. The fact that she was born in Ireland which was in union with the United Kingdom at that time, made Kitty doubt her claim to relief but this was admitted, and for a short time she was given two shillings a week for her children.

Once again she was obliged to work collecting manure, and doing part-time domestic work, or anything else that she could find to look after her family. She knew only too well that her own strength and strong character were the only weapons she possessed to keep the doors of the workhouse at a distance. This stood like a vulture at the top of Brownlow Hill, a spectre which hung over Kitty and the rest of her community. A steady stream of people were going to her most days for help mainly in practical ways. However she was not always able to keep all of them out of the workhouse. It was the children Kitty was most concerned about, as she knew from her own experience what lay in store for them in servitude in the dark satanic mills. There would be times when Kitty felt the pain of seeing children and parents having to go into the workhouse, knowing that neither she nor anybody else, could not do anything to stop this happening.

Meanwhile Kitty was still going out charring, and when offered food during the day Kitty would ask if she could take it home with her to eat later. However her employers knew only too well why she did this, it was so she could share it with her mother and children, such was the poverty of Kitty's household during this time. One or two friends from the Church she attended would give her the flowers from their gardens, which Kitty sold on a Saturday to buy extra food.

It would be very easy to feel Kitty's life was one of sheer gloom, but this was far from the truth as she was very happy and had a cheerful disposition. It was during this period in her life that she started to do some domestic work for the family of Mr. and Mrs. Alexander Braik, trading as Dye's at 6 Pit Street. Whenever they were busy and needed extra help they would call on Kitty. The Braik family were practising Methodists and very caring people who had adopted an orphan girl. At meal times Mr. and Mrs. Braik, together with their children, would eat with the servants. They were known to say that: "Our Lord always ate with His disciples".

Kitty, despite all her problems in looking after her own family and neighbours, was also drawn into helping Mrs. Braik in her charitable work. Whenever Kitty came across a family in need she would let Mrs. Braik know of their circumstances, and Mrs. Braik would pay them a visit. She would also visit the sick, read to them, say some prayers and, before leaving, give them some money, wrapped in paper.

The hard work and sober habits of Kitty started to pay off and she was able to rent a small house in Denison Street. Her Unitarian friends, both rich and poor were delighted for her but they knew she would use her extra accommodation to help others worse off than herself. A poor widow by the name of Mary Powell, who had been a friend of Kitty's mother, was dismissed from the workhouse sometime in 1818. The woman had no place to live and Kitty, seeing her in such a destitute condition, took her into her own home. The woman was deaf and gradually became blind, but for the first eighteen months living with Kitty, Mary Powell was able to earn a little towards her keep.

Once again the tide changed in favour of Kitty as she started to reach middle age. Ten years had passed since her husband had died leaving her with two children and a disabled mother to look after. Kitty was thirty-eight when a new man came into her life. He was Thomas Wilkinson employed as a porter in Mr. William Rathbone's cotton warehouse in Liverpool. After a short courtship Thomas and Kitty were married. Their wedding took place at Holy Trinity Church in Liverpool on the 1st December 1823. He was unable to read or write, so his name was entered for him, followed by his mark. Kitty signed her own name Catherine Demontee, the witnesses to the marriage were William Fisher and Mary Powell.

Thomas was nine years younger than Kitty and it would seem unlikely they would have been friends when they were both at Caton Mill. Kitty was eighteen when she left the apprentice house to live in the village of Caton. Thomas, at the end of each working day, would have been back to the apprentice house, so the chance of any contact between him and Kitty would have been very remote. Thomas was living in Frederick Street when he met Kitty. This was where Kitty lived for a short while on her return from Caton and in all probability Kitty and Thomas would have known one another from living there and from being members of the same Church. He was regarded as a good and honest man with qualities similar to those of Kitty and he was more than willing to share in the responsibility of looking after Kitty's mother and the two children. He was also prepared to take on the burden of attending to Mary Powell, who continued to live with them, In time she became completely dependent on Kitty who continued to nurse her for many years, even though she had her own mother and children to care for.

A few weeks after they were married, Mrs. Jones, a neighbour, asked Kitty if she could attend to one of her children who had been taken ill. Kitty did not know Mrs. Jones very well but, shortly after, she also attended the woman herself when she also became very ill. Sadly Mrs. Jones never recovered from her illness and died a couple of weeks later. She left four children and no relations to look after them. Kitty spoke to Thomas about the situation and he agreed they should take the children. He said he would be prepared to cut down on food himself if need be, and also work longer hours. They accepted responsibility for the four children, and looked after them as though they were their own. The eldest was a girl, who later married, and the second girl turned out to be a great help to Kitty in the house. The other two children were boys, the eldest eventually went to sea and the second boy went into the Bluecoat School, which took in orphan children and gave them an education.

Shortly after accepting responsibility for Mrs Jones' children, Kitty and Thomas took in two more orphan boys. They were not very strong, but with love and care the Wilkinsons soon nursed them back to health. The boys were later apprenticed and were employed by a Captain Finley who was a friend of Kitty and Thomas. He owned his own ship and was prepared to take charge of orphans who were not afraid of hard work. Captain Finley eventually lost his life, being washed overboard from his ship in a heavy storm.

The sea was the major means of employment for Liverpool men. Becoming a seaman would seem be a natural thing for a boy to want to do. There was a great loss of life at sea in those days as ships were only a fraction of the size they are now and far less stable and at the mercy of the elements to a much greater extent than today.

A couple of years after Thomas's marriage to Kitty they had managed to save some money, and were persuaded by a Patrick Dunn to move into a larger house. He was a widower with three small children, who was in full time employment and agreed to pay twenty-four shillings a week for board and lodgings for himself and his children. Patrick was a Roman Catholic, but his late wife had been a Protestant and he promised her the children should be brought up in her faith. After her death he took the children regularly to his wife's church to honour his promise. He lived with the Wilkinsons for seven years and worked in a foundry until the end of his life. Because Patrick Dunn was a Roman Catholic, Kitty always provided him with fish on Fridays, and observed the rituals that his religion demanded of him. Her final act of kindness to him was to send for a priest when she realised he was dying. Kitty is reported to have said: "People go fastest to heaven their own way". So once again Kitty had three more orphans to look after, the youngest boy went into the Bluecoat School and finished up as a seaman.

The girl whose name was Betsy, went into service and was later to marry Kitty's own son John Demontee. The eldest boy was apprenticed at sea, but was unsuited to this pursuit. As they did not want him to become a labourer, they found a place for him in the drawing school of the Mechanics' Institute in order to improve his chances in the trade of carver and gilder. Thomas and Kitty continued to take orphans and other homeless people into their home for years to come. Whenever it was possible they would send the children to the Bluecoat School to be educated. Thomas knew the value of education no matter how limited, having himself been denied a basic education.

It is a sad reflection on society that then, as now, in spite of all the good work Kitty and her husband did in their community, their contribution was not fully appreciated by their contemporaries. By 1828, Kitty and Thomas were still looking after Kitty's mother, who must have been a great age by now. Kitty herself was in her mid-forties, which would in itself be considered as old at that time. Her mother's health was causing Kitty and Thomas some distress, but they continued to look after her rather than have her committed to the Workhouse. Hospitals were non-existent and medication was no more than basic.

As well as the constant worry of her mother, Kitty had to

look after her invalid second younger son, who had been in poor health from the day he was born. His life, however, was drawing to a close and after his death Kitty considered it a merciful release, but she was unable to sleep or eat for some time afterwards. However, with so much sickness in her community people were still knocking on her door. They were desperate, especially those living in the cellars without running water, making it difficult for people to look after themselves. The courts that Kitty had watched being built alongside Denison Street over the years, were not much better than the cellars. The only water supplied was just one standpipe in the courtyard to serve many households.

By 1830 the commerce of the town was thriving and the rich continued to abandon residing in the town. Living in the gentle pastures of the countryside was more conducive to their lifestyle and as wealthy merchants moved out, the poor were still pouring into the town looking for work. However there were a few merchants with genuine concern for the plight of the poor working people of the town, especially those who had come to know Kitty. By 1832 Liverpool was still a very small borough, bound by the Mersey, the outer reaches of the town being Boundary Street in the north and Parliament Street in the south.

At the start of the New Year of 1832 a notable event took place in the lives of the Liverpool merchant class, with a visit from the musical prodigy, Nicolo Paganini, the great Italian violinist. He gave three concerts at the beginning of January in the Theatre Royal, Williamson Square, followed by three others. However his reputation for high admission charges caused much comment by many Liverpool ladies who donated much of their time to charitable work. Their concern was that the lowest price in the gallery was five shillings. Paganini did, however, make some amends by donating his services at a concert on January 30th for the relief of the poor.

The New Year as with other New Years before, did not start well for thousands of poor in the town. Apart from the little charity coming from middle-class ladies, little or no relief came to them from any other quarter. Poor children, many of them in bare feet, had no alternative but to play in dirty, cold streets. A warm January day would be a luxury but cold days also had the single advantage, at least, of keeping some germs at bay. Kitty and her husband, Thomas Wilkinson, were still living in Denison Street involved in helping their community. Workers for the new docks and warehouses needed to be housed as near to their place of work as possible. During the time the courts were being built, people were still moving into cellars throughout Liverpool, and the majority of these cellars had three or four families living in them. The courts were constructed in the shape of a horseshoe, with the entrance through a narrow passage. On each side of courts (which were built back to back) there were four or five houses each with three small rooms. The courtyards were approximately nine to fifteen feet wide, the houses themselves had little ventilation and the refuse was collected on an ad hoc basis. Facing the entrance were the privies (toilets) constructed without running water. There were usually only two, or at most three, privies serving a court which had to cater for as many as twenty families constantly using them, some of the privies even had doors missing. At irregular intervals the contents of the privy would be moved sometimes after it had been full for days. Very little sunshine penetrated the houses due to the narrowness of the courts and the only way people could get fresh air was by standing outside in the courtyard. People had little choice between the smells inside the house and the stench outside. A single standpipe, in each courtyard was the only way to obtain water. It is recorded that the water supply was turned on once or twice a day; according to some reports it was only on alternate days.

Houses in Denison Street all had running water, so it would seem that the water companies would have had little difficulty in supplying water to the courts which were adjacent to this street. Kitty's involvement in her community was known to other members of her church and those who had a more comfortable lifestyle tried to help where they could. Although Kitty was not a member of the privileged class she had come to the notice of William Rathbone and his wife Elizabeth. Mrs. Rathbone with one or two other ladies gave the lead in encouraging other women of her class to join in helping the poor. However well-meaning the efforts of these women, they could not change the minds of those who controlled the water supply to the town, or the private landlords who built slum housing.

As the winter of 1832 was giving way to the onset of spring, news was beginning to filter through that all was not well in the poorer districts of Europe. Cholera had been reported in many areas and by April the first sign of it was evident in Liverpool. Great panic had spread throughout Liverpool and it was not only the poor who feared for their lives, but also many of the middle-class who worked and lived alongside the poor. With the help of her husband, Kitty worked day and night to try and combat the nightmare that had erupted all around them. The signs of what was to come must have been all too clear to Kitty, for she had been actively involved with those who were homeless and sick for most of her life. The fact that she was living in Denison Street before the outbreak of cholera seems to show her lot in life was a little better than most, yet her concern was always for those who were worse off.

Kitty had access to running water and more comforts than most of the neighbours so the combination of water and her humanity were the catalyst of her life-saving efforts on behalf of her neighbours.

She was a true Christian, one who had time for those less well off than herself, and a devout member of her church. She would help anybody, no matter who they were, or what religion they practised, being in need was the only qualification that mattered to her. Kitty attempted to combat the cholera by using clean hot water, which she had brought to a boiling point in the large boiler she had installed in her cellar and actively encouraged her neighbours to wash their bedding and clothes. Cholera is an acute infectious disease and infection usually occurs from drinking contaminated water. The first abrupt symptom is profuse diarrhoea, often accompanied by vomiting. This may lead to rapid loss of fluid and salts, causing muscle cramps, severe thirst and cold, wrinkled skin. If lost fluids were not replaced, coma and death may follow within twenty-four hours.

The cholera hung like a thick black cloud over the town and

people had no place to turn from the terror, which haunted them. This was a challenge that had to be met, and Kitty took it up at a time when there seemed to be little or no hope. At the height of the cholera epidemic Kitty did not run as many others had done. She stayed and went among her panic-stricken neighbours. She kept calm wherever she went, trying to raise the hopes with those she came in contact with. Kitty, with the full backing of her husband, went into the homes of the sick and dying, to bring not only comfort and advice, but also clean bedding.

Kitty nursed the sick, at a time when others were afraid to go anywhere near them for fear of infection. However by her example she encouraged other women to follow her lead. Somehow, whether by some divine providence or natural ability, Kitty was able to convince people that cleanliness and fresh air was a major part of the answer to combating cholera. Kitty nursed the sick and gave good advice, which was not always welcome. Often people could not see the connection of being told about washing their bedding and clothing, when they were living in such poor homes without water. Kitty attracted the attention of some benevolent people and among the things they supplied was oatmeal, which enabled her to make porridge for those in desperate need. There were occasions when Kitty would be looking after as many as sixty men, women and children. One of Thomas's jobs was to bring home as much milk as he could carry every night after his day's work.

She would often spread bedding on the floor of a vacant room to accommodate families whilst their own homes were being disinfected. Many children were homeless, some without parents because of the cholera and Kitty had the extra burden of trying to house them. Until the cholera disaster, Kitty was unknown to people outside her own community. The local media in general was unconcerned about the plight of the poor. However, her work came to the notice of the District Provident Society who gave her much needed help by providing bedding and clothes. Kitty worked long hours, always putting the needs of the sick and suffering people before herself and her husband. She was, at that time, recovering from an illness herself, and had been warned she would be putting her life in danger if she continued working such long hours. Kitty went ahead fulfilling what she felt to be her duty. Many families were living in a single room without bedding or any of the creature comforts one would normally expect to find even in those times. This was a nightmare that had engulfed Kitty.

However, she devoted all her time, thoughts, and all she possessed in an endeavour to lessen the misery around her. The few doctors on hand could not possibly cope. This was a time before nurses were available so she administered the remedies on the doctors' instructions. Kitty set up a washroom in her kitchen, boiling water in a large copper container in the corner of the room. Then she got Thomas to fix up clotheslines in the yard and invited her poorer neighbours who were without the means of boiling water to wash the infected clothes and bedding. The newly washed garments and bedding could be seen drying in the yard night and day. Another reason for Kitty encouraging people to dry their clothes in her yard, was to make sure their clothes were dried properly.

People would put on damp clothes, not having the proper facilities for drying. This lead by Kitty was probably the turning point in letting people know they should have the right to clean water and better sanitary conditions. By the autumn of the year, 5,000 people had been affected, more than 1,500 people died out of a population of 230,000. The great supporters of Kitty in her praiseworthy efforts were Mr. and Mrs. Rathbone who were already aware of her concern for the poor. She also received great help from Rector Campbell and members of the congregation of her church.

The District Provident Society came to know of Kitty's methods in tackling the cholera outbreak. They gave her the help she needed in providing soap and other assistance for washing cholera infected clothes and bedding. A local Surgeon also called to see Kitty to give her some advice on how infected clothes and bedding might be washed without risk to those engaged in doing it. Kitty was giving the lead in her neighbourhood showing the wider community how to tackle this menace that was taking its toll. Poor people in other parts of Liverpool were having clothes and bedding burned by order of the magistrates, such was the lack of understanding of cholera and its treatment. While all the debating was going on as to the causes of cholera, Kitty was busy combating the disease with clean water and disinfectant. Word soon spread that Mrs Wilkinson in Denison Street had started a washhouse. Kitty contrived to provide for the washing of, on average, eighty-five families per week. People contributed 'one penny per week' to assist in defraying expenses. Kitty collected about twenty orphaned children in her bedroom and a neighbour, Mrs. Lloyd, began to teach them simple hymns and stories and sing to them. The numbers increased and by degrees an infant school was formed without funds or books or chairs for the children to sit on. The help of a benevolent individual, whose name is unknown, gave Kitty assistance in the furtherance of her labour of love. The Corporation also gave further help and the result was a school for one hundred and ninety children. Mrs. Lloyd was rewarded for her good work and leadership by her appointment as headmistress.

Liverpool Corporation, at the time of the epidemic, had not taken any comprehensive responsibility to bring about a water supply for everyone, although as far back as 1786 the council had the powers to supply water. In 1794 the Corporation purchased, from a private concern, some caravans that were based on the north shore and spent £5,000 renovating them. In a marketing pamphlet distributed amongst the genteel members of society in the town, it prescribed the benefits of the caravans: "As commodious, safe, elegant, as any of the kind in England, and having all the advantages of the salubrity of the salt water without exposing the bather to view".

By 1835 life had changed very little for most people and the town was still receiving people looking for work. The new docks and factories were a magnet drawing people from all parts of the United Kingdom. No longer was Liverpool the tiny little town that opened its arms to Kitty in 1790. The dreaded cholera was, however, still showing its ugly head although not to the same degree. Life for the people of Denison Street certainly had not changed for the better. The Street was surrounded by the court system of housing. Great Howard Street at the top of Denison Street and Leeds Street, just the other side of Great Howard Street, also had a number of courts.

Denison Street, Waterloo Road at the bottom end

Kitty's house (on left) in Denison Street
Demolished in 1951

There were courts and alleys attached to Denison Street, Cook's, Scales, Arthur's, Denison and Bell Court.

Kitty's health was still giving cause for alarm, which had not gone unnoticed by Mrs. Rathbone. Kitty was worried about the fate of her eldest son, John Demontee. He had been at sea for some time, his ship was long overdue and the anxiety added to her poor state of health. She had after all every right to be alarmed, for the sea had claimed too many of Kitty's family. Mrs. Rathbone's intervention about Kitty's health sparked off a chain of events that was to give Kitty some reassurance about her son's welfare. She received a letter from Boston, written by Joseph Tuckerman on June 10 1835:

My Dear Mrs. Wilkinson,

I have within a few days received a letter from our friend Mrs. Rathbone, who informs me that, at the date of her letter, you were indisposed, your health a good deal run down by cares and labours. I am concerned to learn this. I do not mean that I feel any of that uneasiness which implies discontent with the government of our Heavenly Father. I shall never forget the hour I spent with you and your orphans. It was a holy hour. It was an hour to be remembered with joy in heaven. I have many delightful recollections of England, but I remember nothing there, which is more sacred in my thoughts and in my heart than the hour I spent in your little parlour.

The name of Kitty Wilkinson and her work for the poor of the town had not gone unnoticed by the town council. In 1846 Liverpool decided it would honour Kitty. She and her husband Thomas were invited to Carnatic Hall which at that time was outside the Liverpool boundary. Kitty had been told that she was to meet Queen Victoria, and other members of the Royal Family. She had no idea her achievement in combating cholera and work for the poor had come to the notice of the Queen. Also present at Carnatic Hall was Mr George Lawrence, the Mayor of Liverpool. Queen Victoria presented Kitty with a silver tea service, which included a teapot engraved with the words:

'The Queen the Queen Dowager and the Ladies of Liverpool to Catherine Wilkinson 1846.'

Kitty was sixty years of age at this time and still had a lot of energy. This was also when she and Thomas were offered the position of superintendents of the new washhouse at 135 Upper Frederick Street. Taking up this appointment could not have been easy for Kitty, as it meant leaving Denison Street where she had spent most of her life. Denison Street had been the springboard for most of her work, the street where the world's first public washhouse came into being. The post of superintendent of the new washhouse came about through the intervention of William Rathbone.

Thomas Wilkinson was a humble and hard working man who appeared to spend his life helping other people and he must have felt very proud when, in 1846, he and Kitty were appointed Superintendents of the Corporation Baths. At last the Wilkinsons were enjoying some of the fruits of life. Kitty and Thomas showed the same level of commitment working in the new establishment as they did in 1832 when fighting the cholera, and being paid for serving the community was like a bonus.

They no longer had the burden of looking after a family. Mrs Seaward had passed on, but the painful memories of Kitty losing her youngest son still lingered. John, the seagoing son, was married with a family living in Stockport and the last of her orphans had left to make their own way in life. However they still had their friends and the friendship and respect of William Rathbone and his family. The Unitarian Church still played a big part in their lives which helped to fill the void in their much slower lifestyle despite the responsibilities of running the new Corporation Baths.

Many changes with improvements and amenities were taking place in the town much to Kitty's delight. She would surely have been pleased when Dr Duncan was appointed to be Liverpool's first Medical Officer of Health in 1846 shortly after her own appointment. Just a few months later the first Borough Engineer, Mr. James Newlands, was appointed and took up his post in February 1847. He brought about sewers, a better drainage system and the first connection of house drains to sewers. This made possible the substitution of water closets for the privies and middens, which we now know, contributed so much to disease.

The new baths and washhouse was packed every day with women doing their family washing, many of them coming from other areas. This facility allowed people to do their washing in comfort with no restriction on the amount of water used. The washhouse also brought a comradeship amongst women, which allowed them to express their feelings. It allowed them to escape from the drudgery of bad housing provided by private landlords and a chance to get away from husbands and children for a few hours. Domestic servants from big houses also made use of the facilities for their employers. Many wealthy people living in the town would not have had facilities as good as those provided at the washhouse. What Kitty had created in her home in 1832 was to be repeated in every major town throughout the British Isles and many countries in Europe. In Scotland the washhouses became known as "steamies".

The joy and pleasure the Wilkinsons derived from seeing people improve their lives, did not last long. People were fleeing the famine in Ireland and landing in the town from every type of vessel. We may never know for sure if Kitty played a part in helping to ease the suffering of the famine victims. However it would be hard to imagine she did not involve herself. Many would have used the washhouse and lived alongside her. It is more than possible that Kitty would have taken some new arrivals into her home, after all she had been caring for her neighbours most of her life.

Kitty had been greatly encouraged in her devotion to the community by Thomas throughout their marriage. He was the man behind a great woman. However, sadly less than two years after his appointment of joint superintendent of the washhouse, Thomas took ill at home in 70 Upper Frederick Street with bronchitis. Kitty's son, John, was home from sea and staying with the family at the time. Thomas never recovered from his illness and died 31 December 1849. (Note: John De-Monte was the informant at the time of death on 31 December, 1849. Also the name Demontee had been changed to De-monte.) The man who had been by her side through one of the blackest periods in Liverpool's history was laid to rest in St. James's Cemetery. Not for the first time in her life, Kitty was alone.

Gore's Street Directory in 1858 listed Kitty as a boarding keeper at 70, Upper Frederick Street. She was living just doors from the "The Kitty Wilkinson Baths and Wash-house" which was still serving the community. People were still passing Kitty's with their bundles of dirty washing perched on their heads. If lucky, they would have some sort of contraption on wheels to carry it. Not many poor women would have had a pram for their babies, so chances of having an old one were remote. Kitty would have observed the women later returning with their clean clothes and bedding. Almost thirty years had passed since the first signs of cholera brought death and misery to the area. The name of Kitty would mean very little to those people still arriving from Wales, Ireland, Scotland and many areas of Lancashire and Cheshire.

In 1859 Kitty's health was a cause for concern. She was not too well at the beginning of the year and went to convalesce at the home of Mrs Gilbertson. On her return home, Kitty composed a short letter to this lady and it is clear from reading this that Kitty's mind and intellect were very intact. Letter written by Kitty to Mrs Gilbertson, February 2, 1869:

> Would you be so kind as to gather my things for me, you will find them in the bedroom where I slept and send them by the Cart tomorrow for I am very ill and will not be able to come out for them, and please to let me know how Mrs. Paget is and John's wife for I am very uneasy about her, remember me to all and let me know how Ibison Hand is and how you are, for I feel a deal worse since I came home, for I dare not go near the door no more at present from.
> Catherine Wilkinson

Kitty's life at this time was slowly ebbing away, the strength of this great woman was leaving her body, like the sap leaving a great tree, alone in a forest. Gone were the sea of faces that had passed through her hands, the orphans and the sick, which she nursed and guided through life. There was no great newspaper correspondent writing to "The Times Newspaper' to tell the world about this most wonderful woman. It was left to the Liverpool newspapers to inform the rest of the country that it was Kitty Wilkinson who fought the cholera almost single handed, until she was helped in her task by Mr. and Mrs. Rathbone. Her work amongst the poor must have planted the seeds of progress into the minds of other men and women from other towns and other countries. Kitty Wilkinson died on 11 November 1860, and present at the time of her death was a friend of hers, Mary Lawson. Mary could not write her own name, so the death certificate gave the mark of Mary Lawson of 39 Jordan Street.

Kitty was interred on Wednesday, 14 November 1860 at St. James's Cemetery. Present were William Rathbone and many of her adopted children. However her son, John Demontee, did not go. It could have been that word of his mother's death had not reached him at his home in Stockport. We know that John was a seaman so it is possible that he was on the high seas. Mr. Shimming of Pit Street made arrangements for the funeral.

In its obituary column, Gores General Advertiser, 22 November, 1860 reported the death of Catherine Wilkinson. 'The inventor of Wash-Houses for the poor.'

Just over seven years after the death of Kitty, Mr. William Rathbone, the man who had played such a vital role in her work, died aged 80 on 1 February 1868. at his home, Greenbank, Liverpool, and was buried at Smithdown Lane Cemetery. After his death, a statue of William was erected by public subscription in Sefton Park, Liverpool. His wife Margaret survived him by fifteen years.

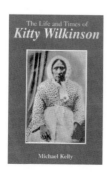

*First Edition
in 2000*

*Second Edition
in 2007*

Chapter 19

$\mathcal{S}$arah $\mathcal{B}$iffen

$\mathcal{Q}$uite often we describe people by their physical features, tall, short, fair or dark and we accept these descriptions as the norm. However there are people who we sometimes regard as being physically disabled and we will describe them in that way, without knowing the person. Sarah Biffen was born into a world where her appearance was different from those of her parents and neighbours but her name and ability as a great painter still lives on long after her death a hundred and fifty-year ago.

Sarah was born on October 25th 1784 in the small village of East Quantoxhead, Somerset. Her parents Henry and Sarah Biffen, already had two sons, one of whom did not survive, and two more daughters. They must have been shocked and grieved when their first daughter whom they named Sarah, was born without arms or legs. At that time such children were likely to be regarded by their parents with shame and their fate was grim.

A kindly old clergyman visited Biffen's cottage, inspected

the child, who was entirely limbless though otherwise perfectly healthy, and ultimately baptised her "Sarah," after her mother, with strict injunctions that she was to be treated merely as a crippled child. She grew up in the squalid surroundings of a farm labourer's cottage, and showed remarkable intelligence at an early age. Unable to walk, she learned to roll and trundle herself about. She could pick up things with her mouth, and acted normally.

The fame of the child spread far and wide, and from being a burden she became a source of revenue for her parents. The vicar of East Quantoxhead, near Bridgewater, where Sarah was born, taught her to read; and, once she knew her letters, Sarah taught herself to write by holding a pencil in her mouth and, in a lot of pain, copied words onto paper. By the time she was seven, Sarah Biffen could read and write, and this was a rare accomplishment for a West Country farm labourer's daughter. Whenever a newspaper arrived from Bath or Bristol, she would often be taken in a barrow to the local inn. There she would read the news aloud to the farm labours of the execution of Marie Antoinette, and other tragedies and events of the French Revolution.

Although they appeared kind, the village children, just like their fathers and mothers, really treated Sarah badly and regarded her as a "pixie child" (a small fairy). Had it not been for the benevolent clergyman, her childhood would indeed have been an unhappy one. He placed the books in the rectory library at her disposal. She read them avidly and grew wise beyond her years. Then she started to copy engravings and woodcuts and was soon able to draw and sketch. When she was 12, Sarah arrived at the height of 37 inches and never grew taller, although her body became that of a woman in proportion to her size.

An acquaintance of Sarah's father, a Mr. Dukes, came one day to Quantoxhead and watched little Sarah write and draw with great interest. He next sought out George Biffen, her father, whom he accompanied to the village inn, where, over mugs of cider, followed by ale, they had a deep and lengthy conversation. Eventually money was pressed into Biffen's hand, who promptly shambled from his seat and returned to his cottage, where, after consultation, Sarah agreed to bind herself to Mr. Dukes for sixteen years, in return for £5 per annum and he agreed to pay for all she needed to keep her in health.

From that moment Sarah became the man's slave. He conveyed her all over the country from fair to fair, where she was exhibited as 'The Limbless Wonder' in a booth where, according to locality, 3p to 5p was charged for admission. Perched upon a pedestal, with a kind of easel beside her, Sarah used to write her autograph for 1p, and write letters at dictation from 3p each, according to their length, draw crayon portraits, and paint little landscapes. Dukes made large sums by exhibiting her, and he overworked her shamefully and even compelled her to paint landscapes and portraits of celebrities on Sundays, which he sold for considerable amounts. This went on until, at the age of 28, Sarah's sixteen years of servitude expired.

Strange to say, at the very last place she was exhibited as the 'The Limbless Wonder', fortune for the first time smiled upon poor Sarah Biffen at Swaffam Race Week in 1812. Here Lord Morton and some friends paid their shillings and entered the booth to see 'The Limbless Wonder' paint miniature portraits for two to three guineas, and perform other extraordinary exploits with brush and pen held in her mouth. He was amazed at her ability, entered into conversation with her and heard her life story, with the result that, as her contract with Dukes was on the point of expiring, he took her away and arranged further art training for her by a famous portrait painter and illustrator of the period, named Joseph Craig. Under this tuition, Sarah progressed rapidly and several exhibitions of her work in art galleries followed, her watercolours fetching high prices.

George IV and William IV visited and purchased her pictures. Eventually in 1821 she was awarded the Gold Medal of the Society of Arts, when commissions commenced to pour upon her. Having miniatures painted on ivory was almost as popular at that period as having one's photograph taken is now, and for some years Sarah Biffen earned good money. Later she attracted the attention of Queen Victoria, who always took a great interest in out-of-the-ordinary people. Her Majesty's patronage of Van Ambergh, the lion tamer, and of Tom Thumb, is well known, and as soon as she heard that Miss Biffen, the fashionable miniature painter, was a limbless artist, she expressed a desire to see her. Sarah was then commissioned to paint miniature portraits of the late King Edward and his sister, who afterwards became the ex-Kaiser's mother.

Soon after this, Sarah left London and resided in Liverpool, where for some years she made a profitable living by her art. Then, as old age commenced to creep on her, she began to lose control over the muscles of her neck and mouth, which were, of course, highly developed. Valiantly, she struggled, but overwork exacted its toll and she gradually lost control and became almost unable to paint. She struggled bravely on for some years. Debts accumulated, and finally the poor little artist succumbed to poverty again.

Creditors pressed, and finally she was destitute. The strain on her neck and labial muscles distorted her once pretty face and she looked old and haggard. She had arrived at the stage when she was still talked about by the older generation but forgotten by the younger people. Mr. Richard Rathbone, a member of the firm of artists' colourmen who used to supply her in her better days with the paints and pigments she used in her work, raised a fund and was successful in obtaining sufficient money for this brave little limbless woman to be at peace once more.

So, Sarah Biffen did not have to end her days as a freak at country fairs, as she had when she commenced her career, or become an inmate of the workhouse, which in her day and generation, as all readers of Dickens know, was an abode of dread. Fortunately she was spared from these fates. Sarah's health deteriorated during the following three years and she died on 2nd October 1850, three weeks before her 66th birthday. She was buried in St James Cemetery, now St James Gardens behind Liverpool Anglican Cathedral. In 1824 she was reported to have married a man by the name of Wright but little is known of him. Her death certificate states she was the widow of 'Wright, bankers clerk'. It is believed they never lived together, but she defended him against those who said that he took her money and deserted her. Sarah said that for as long as he was able he allowed her £40 per annum.

In Windsor Castle there is a miniature, which she painted of Edward Duke of Kent, father of Queen Victoria. This was a copy of a portrait by George Dawe, so it would seem that she was permitted to visit Windsor to work; two of her miniatures are in the Victoria and Albert Museum. It is believed that Sarah was granted a civil-list pension of £12 per annum by William 1V, no date is given but it continued until her death. She visited many places around the country, which must have been very difficult for her, considering her disability and the only way to travel would have been by horse drawn carriage over rough roads. She visited Brighton, Cheltenham, Exeter, Oxford and many other towns around the country, before coming to Liverpool in 1841.

Sarah seemed to have had trouble settling down, living at different addresses during her early days in the town. Liverpool's economy at that time was going through a lean time, and many of the smaller traders and shopkeepers were finding it difficult to keep their heads above water. Although she would have been known to those in the more cultured circles, her popularity may have been on the wane and her advancing years and infirmity would not have helped her, resulting in fewer orders.

Her circumstance had not gone unnoticed amongst the gentry of the town. In 1847 Richard Rathbone, one of the sons of William Rathbone and a family who were noted philanthropists, issued an appeal for funds to buy her an annuity. The Queen Dowager and other members of the Royal Family headed the subscription list. It included the Earls of Sefton and Ellesmere, Le Prince de Joinville, Jenny Lind and the actor/manager Mcready. Theodore Rathbone arranged for the erection of a tombstone with a long inscription, which now appears to have been destroyed. In 1939, 'London Life' Magazine published the following:

Marvellous Feats Of Limbless People from miniature painting to tiger shooting. Believe it or not, but among the art treasures at Windsor Castle and Buckingham Palace are exquisite miniatures of members of the Royal family painted by Miss Sarah Biffen, who was entirely limbless.

Yet though born without hands, without even rudimentary arms or legs, her skill with pencil and brush wielded in her mouth gives her a place in Redgrave's 'Dictionary of British Artists' and the still greater honour of inclusion in the company of Reynolds and Turner, Romney, Millais and Sargent in that most austere of reference books, 'The Dictionary of National Biography'.

Sarah was well known in the literary world, and was referred to by name by Thomas Hood in the 'The Mermaid of Margate', Charles Dickens in 'Nicholas Nickleby', 'Martin Chuzzlewit', 'Little Dorrit', 'Surtees' and 'Handley Cross'. Horace Smith wrote a jocular account of a visit by her to Covent Garden Theatre, and Thomas Rowlandson included her in a sketch of the attractions of 'Bartholomew Fair'. But she lived to paint Edward VII and the Ex-Kaiser's mother.

"Aye, thou can coom in now, Garge Biffen, it's a girl. And marcy on us, what a girl!", said the matronly looking, poorly clad woman as she opened the door of the sleeping room, which was feebly lighted by two flickering rushlights, and admitted George Biffen, the father of the new-born child. "An' how be Sarah, Mary?" he asked, in the slow but not unmusical drawl of the Somersetshire rustics. "Finely", was the reply. "She be just a-droppin' off to sleep, so don't wake 'er, Garge." Garge nodded. His slow brain comprehended that sleep was his wife's best medicine. "An' the babby, Mary?" as a faint cry came from the bed where the woman was lying. "Sarah be a cuddlin' it up to her," said the woman called Mary, who was George Biffen's sister.

"You won't blame it on her, will 'e, Garge? It baint poor Sarah's fault! When I took the baby from 'er it was a small sized un, too. I thought I'd died! Garge, it 'as no limbs. I fear the pixies 'ave lopped 'em off!" The yokel's slow brain found difficulty in comprehending his sister's statement. "No limbs?" he muttered. "D'yer mane no arms an' no legs?" "Yes, Garge." "God in 'eaven! Then 'ow can the kid work for its livin'? Mary you should have smothered it afore Sarah saw it. It be a pixie, sure enough!" "I thought so, too," said his trembling sister, "but I was feared, mort'ly feared!

The law, Garge - the law!" "Feared?" said the man. "It'd be a marcy."

"So I thought; but it 'as sich a pretty little face and, Garge, it'd be murder!" "Maybe so," said her brother, "but summat 'ad to be done. I'll step down to the village and ask parson wot's to do." This wise decision of her father saved, in all probability, the limbless mite's life. Strange to say, at the very last place she was exhibited as the "The Limbless Wonder", Fortune for the first time smiled upon poor Sarah Biffen.

There can be no doubt that the achievements of Sarah Biffen will have played a part in helping the general public to understand the many qualities that disabled people have.

Artist Marc Quinn paid tribute to his friend Alison Lapper in a public ceremony with his sculpture, 'Alison Lapper Pregnant' which was unveiled by Mayor Ken Livingstone, in Trafalgar Square, London. Alison was born without arms and with shortened legs. Quinn's work is a portrait of her when she was eight months pregnant.

Miniature painted on ivory

Chapter 20

&llen &ate

*W*e live in an age where we expect people to live to a great age with the help of science, medication and hospital care. It is said that a characteristic of civilised nations, is to venerate age, whether the individuals are 'Fluent in rags, or flutter in brocade'. Mrs. Ellen Tate was an example of longevity in the 18th, and 19th centuries at a time when most poor people died before the age of twenty-five. Ellen was born in 1713 in the parish of Killede, County Antrim. Her maiden name was Craig, but little is known of her family and early life. She was married to a schoolmaster, whose name was Tate and by whom she had four children. Two of them died at an early age and one became a mariner who sailed out of Liverpool and made the town his home after moving from County Antrim.

Ellen's husband had died when her children were still quite young, and she was living alone after her two remaining children had moved out to make a life for themselves. It was very lonely for Ellen in her cottage in Killede, then her mariner son sent for her to move with him to a house he had in the port of Liverpool. Ellen looked after his house and her son's affairs when he was away on a voyage. Her new life in the town soon started to blossom when she became a member of a local Church and made many new friends. Ellen became a part of the respectable society of the growing seaport and was often invited to afternoon tea by her Church-going friends.

Sadly her comfortable life fell apart with the death of her son who drowned at sea. When she reached sixty in 1773, a great age in those days, not having any means of her own, she had to support herself by doing any job that came along in the market. There was no pension or state help in those days and Ellen was thankful for anything that came her way. After her job in the market failed due to lack of work she took to the streets with a basket on her head, containing religious tracks, laces and ribbons and other pieces of haberdashery.

Ellen continued to support herself in this fashion for more than thirty years, sooner than place herself at the mercy of the parish. Sadly the day came when she was to old to be walking the streets selling her goods and there was little profit in her occupation, so she was forced to apply to the parish as the last resort.

She was ninety-four at the time of entering the workhouse and soon became a favourite of the governor. Despite her great age she was in good health and had a highly retentive memory. She was allowed to visit the town centre when the mood took her and as the years passed on she became more of a curiosity with passers by in the town who saw her smoking her clay pipe. Because of her advanced years she was allowed an extra allowance of tea, some ale and other comforts, supplied by the workhouse governor.

Strangers and the gentry who occasionally visited the workhouse, viewed her with veneration, and frequently gave her money. Ellen was still attending church at the time of her hundredth birthday, and eventually lived for another ten years, dying at the age of hundred and ten, in 1823.

Bibliography

Beaven, Margaret.
Margaret Beavan of Liverpool Her Character and Work, by IVY A. Ireland.
Published by Henry Yong & Sons Ltd 1938, Margaret Beavan, 'The Little Mother Of Liverpool', A dissertation by Janet Mclarney, B. A. (Lancaster) University of Lancaster, October 1995.
Eleanor Rathbone and the Politics of Citizenship. Author: Field, Frank. Source: The Political Quarterly, Volume 76, Number 2 April 2005, pp. 171-180.

Biffen, Sarah
Freak Show to Court Favourite, Country Life.
19 September 1985.

Braddock, Bessie
New York Times, 28 March 1952.
Illustrated London News 4 March 1950.
The Times, 9 May 1955.
Who's Who, 1957.
Bessie Braddock, Liverpool Echo special edition,
17 November 1987.

Butler, Josephine
The Josephine Butler Memorial Lecture, by Margaret Simey,
16 March 1995.
Biographical sketches of memorial Christians, Josephine Butler,
Pioneer Worker Among Women, 30 December 1906.
Josephine Butler, by Jane Jordan published by John Murray 2001.
Liverpool University, special collections, Josephine Butler
Collection, reference No. GB 141 JBC.

Crosbie, Jessie Reid, M.B.E., M.A.
This Kingdom Called Home, by Jessie Reid Crosbie. Published by Phillip & Nephew, Liverpool, 1954.
My Liverpool, by Frank Shaw, Wolf Publishing LTD, 1971.
1881 British Census, Dwelling 27 Copley Street, Public Records Office reference RG11, piece/folio 3665/103, page number 61.

Dod, Lottie
Champion of Champions, by Jeffrey Pearson. The Story of an Athlete. Published by Countyvise Ltd, Birkenhead 1988.

Hemans, Felicia
Saxon, Think Not All is Won.
Jane Arron, Felicia Hemans and The Making of Britons.
The Liverpool Homes, of Mrs. Hemans by George T.Shaw, Master and Librarian of the Athenaeum Liverpool. Hon. Librarian of the Historic Society of Lancashire and Cheshire.
Liverpool, F. & E. Gibbons, 10, Ranelagh Street,1897.
Moral And Religious Quotations From The Poets Topically Arranged: Comprising Choice Selection. From Six Hundred Authors. Compiled by Rev. William Rice, A.M. Seventh Edition. New York: Published by Carlton & Porter, 1804.
Memorials of Mrs. Hemans, by Henry F. Chorley in two volumes, London, Saunders and Otley, 1836.
Mrs. Hugh's memoir in collective edition, 1839.
E. W. Whately's Remarkable People, 1889.
The Streets Of Liverpool, by James Stonehouse.

Heilbron, Dame Rose
Pioneer in legal profession, by Larry Neild, Liverpool Daily Post, 13 December 2005.
Obituary Liverpool Daily Post 16 September 2004
Obituary Telegraph 12 December 2005.
The Legal Executive, Journal of the Institute of Legal Executives, 25 November 2007.

Jones, Agnes.
A Gifted Touch, by James Cosbie Ross and John Ross, published 1988.
Memorials of Agnes Elizabeth Jones, by her Sister 1871. Published by Strahan & CO.
Noble Women of Our Time, By Joseph Johnson, 1883.
Northern Ireland Hospitals, North-West Management Committee. 6 April 1954.
Liverpool The Irish Connection, by Michael Kelly, published by Print Origination, Formby 2003.

Kelly, Margaret
Bluebell, by George Perry, published by Prime Productions Ltd 1986.
The Courage of Miss Bluebell, Sharon Wright, Daily Express, 16 September 2004.
Obituary, Liverpool Daily Post, 16 September 2004.

Simey, Margaret
The Josephine Butler Memorial Lecture 16th March 1995. Liverpool John Moores University.
Raymond Clark, Guardian. Obituary 29 July 2004.

Thom, Mary Hannah.
'My Parish Holy Cross' by Margaret Donnelly. Published by Starfish Multimedia.
Liverpool Weekly Mercury, 11 January 1908.
Liverpool University, Sidney Jones Library, John Hamilton Thom (1816-1872).
RP X111.1 – General correspondence (146 item).
RPX111.2 – Personal papers.

Whitty, Dame May
Dame of the Theatre by Eric Johns, Arlington House, New York 1974.
The Same Only Different by Margaret Webster London, Victor Gollancz LTD 1969.
Liverpool The Irish Connection, by Michael Kelly published by Print Origination Formby 2003.
Liverpool's Irish Connection, by Michael Kelly, AJH Publishing, Formby UK 2006.

Wilkinson, Kitty
The Life and Times of Kitty Wilkinson, by Michael Kelly, published by Countyvise, 2000, and second edition 2007.